Aunt Phil's Trunk: Volume 4

An Alaska historian's collection of treasured tales

By
Phyllis Downing Carlson
Laurel Downing Bill

Aunt Phil's Trunk LLC
Anchorage, Alaska

www.auntphilstrunk.com

The front cover design by Kristy Bernier of Palmer, Alaska, features Phyllis Downing Carlson, aunt of Laurel Downing Bill, prior to her death in 1993.

Carlson grew up in Alaska and wrote numerous magazine and newspaper articles about the state she loved.

Also on the cover, from left: Natives at Unalakleet, Alaska State Library, Mabel and Emil Fisher Collection, ASL-P368-89; road signs, Alaska State Library, Alaska Highway Construction Collection, ASL-P193-158; June 30, 1958, newspaper headline, Anchorage Daily Times; and John Ben "Benny" Benson holding his design for the Alaska flag, Alaska State Library, Portrait File, ASL-P01-1921.

International Standard Book Number 1-57833-435-3
Library of Congress Control Number 2006908361

Printed and bound in the United States of America.

First printing 2009

DEDICATION

I dedicate this book to Aunt Phil's stepchildren, grandchildren, great-grandchildren and their families; to Aunt Phil's sister, Jean Downing Anderson of Seward; to my brothers and sisters, their families and all our cousins. I also dedicate the work to my husband, Donald; son Ryan; and daughter Kim and her husband, Bruce Sherry, along with my beautiful granddaughters, Sophia Isobel and Maya Josephine Sherry. Thank you so much for believing in me.

Lastly, I dedicate this collection of historical stories to my faithful readers. Thank you for your support and constant encouragement.

ACKNOWLEDGMENTS

I owe an infinite debt of gratitude to the University of Alaska Anchorage, the University of Alaska Fairbanks, the Anchorage Museum of History and Art, the Alaska State Library in Juneau, the Z.J. Loussac Public Library in Anchorage, the Seward Community Library and the University of Washington for helping me collect the photographs for this book. Without the patient and capable staffs at these institutions, the following pages may not have been filled.

I want to extend a heart-felt thank you to Robert DeBerry of Wasilla for his excellent attention to detail as he readied for publication the historical photographs that appear in Volume 4 of Aunt Phil's Trunk. I also am extremely grateful to Nancy Pounds of Anchorage for slaving away with her eagle eyes to carefully proofread the pages.

My family deserves medals, as well, for putting up with me as I chased down just the right photographs to go with Aunt Phil's stories, poured over notes and the collection of rare books that make up Aunt Phil's library and sat hunched over my computer for hours blending selections of Aunt Phil's work with stories from my own research.

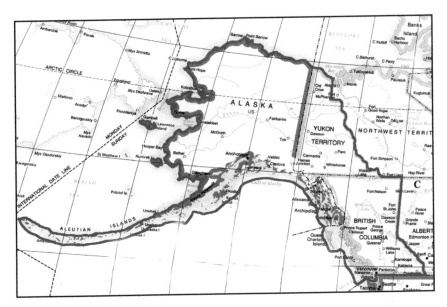

    "Aunt Phil's Trunk: Volume 4" is filled with stories that take the reader from 1935 to 1960. It includes events that unfolded during World War II, the Cold War with Russia and the long struggle for statehood.

Phyllis Downing Carlson, who arrived in Cordova, Alaska, in 1914 at the age of 5, lived and loved the history about which she wrote.

FOREWORD

This book contains a collection of Alaska history stories written by my aunt, Phyllis Downing Carlson, as well as stories written by me that came from tidbits found among the notes and rare books I inherited when she died in 1993.

Born in 1909, Aunt Phil moved to Alaska in 1914 and lived the history so richly described in her work. She grew up in Cordova, where her father worked on building the railroad to the Kennecott copper mines; he then served as the conductor aboard the Copper River and Northwestern Railway. Phyllis graduated with a class of seven from Cordova High School in 1928, then studied journalism at the University of Washington and earned a teacher's certificate from Central College of Education in Ellensburg, Washington.

Aunt Phil landed her first job, which paid a whopping $150 a month, at Cooper Landing on the Kenai Peninsula. The new teacher kept the Yukon stove stoked in the little log schoolhouse and worked around cases of milk and staples stored for the winter.

After three years in the isolated community of 30, a widowed father of three of her pupils put an end to her single days. Carl Carlson moved her to the village of Tyonek, across Cook Inlet from Anchorage, and Phil again taught school in 1935 while Carl ran the village sawmill and served as postmaster.

The young bride met Tyonek Chief Simeon Chickalusion, who spoke English, Russian and his Native tongue. She later wrote an article, titled "The Tribe That Kept Its Head," about the chief and residents of Tyonek that ranked as one of the best articles submitted in a 1967 Writer's Digest contest. Years later, the village invited her back to a potlatch to share stories of the chief with the village young people.

The Carlsons moved to Anchorage in 1939, where Carl helped build Fort Richardson. The couple pitched a tent at Fifth Avenue and Denali Street and started framing a house over the tent. When they completed their home, they took down the tent and dragged it out the front door.

As a child, Alaska historian Phyllis Downing Carlson skipped down the dirt streets in Cordova, pictured here in 1919.

Phyllis Downing Carlson, who grew up in Cordova, taught school in the Native village of Tyonek in 1935. The village looked much like this photograph taken in 1898. She befriended Chief Simeon Chickalusion and was invited back to a potlatch when the village relocated after the village flooded during the 1960s.

After World War II, the couple moved to Cordova, where Aunt Phil honed her journalism skills. She produced her own radio show, "Woman to Woman," and conducted countless interviews that eventually led her to research Cordova's history through the local newspaper's archives.

"Oh, I had a wonderful time," she later recalled. "They had a real storehouse."

Her popular radio show led to the compilation of entertaining articles about Alaska, and for more than 40 years, Aunt Phil researched and wrote award-winning pieces as she moved about the state. Her stories appeared in a multitude of publications, including Alaskana, Alaska Journal, Alaska Sportsman, The Anchorage Times and Our Alaska.

She settled back in Anchorage from Kodiak after the Good Friday earthquake of 1964, and Phil spent so much time researching and talking with librarians at the Z.J. Loussac Public Library, they hired her. People said she didn't need to use the card catalog, because she knew the location of every volume.

"I don't remember faces," she said. "But I remember what I looked up for people."

The Alaska Press Women chose Aunt Phil for its Woman of Achievement Award in 1988. The organization cited her as an authority on Alaska history, recognized throughout the state by writers, researchers and politicians alike.

As a retiree, she served on a variety of boards, including the Anchorage Bicentennial Commission, Historical Landmarks Preservation Commission, State Historical Society and Alaska Press Women.

When she passed away in 1993, her treasured tales landed in my hands. As providence would have it, I, too, am a writer and lover of Alaska history. And since Aunt Phil was one of my favorite relatives, I feel privileged to perpetuate her work.

My Alaska roots stem from both sides of my family. My father, Richard Allie Downing – Aunt Phil's younger brother – was born in Cordova in 1916. Not only was his father a part of the railroad history there, but his grandfather, John Couch Downing, had witnessed the staking of gold claims around the area many years before when he sailed as the captain of the *Excelsior* and the *Portland*, both famous steamships that carried news of the riches found in the Klondike back to San Francisco and Seattle in July 1897.

My mother's grandfather, Robert Burns Mathison, arrived in Hope from Texas in 1898 and helped establish that little mining town. He pulled a small fortune out of Resurrection Creek and Chickaloon River and built a sawmill and mercantile. His son, Robert Lewis Mathison, married my grandmother, Inez Lee Brown, who traveled to the small community to work for her uncle, Charlie Shields, after being widowed in Kansas.

From that union came my mother, Hazel Isobel, and her identical twin, Hope Alisabeth, born at the Anchorage railroad hospital in 1920. The twins spent summers in Hope and winters in Seward, where they graduated high school in 1938.

My parents met at the University of Alaska Fairbanks, married in 1941, and settled in Fairbanks to raise their family. I was the fourth of their children born at old St. Joseph's Hospital, in 1951, following brothers Richard Ellsworth and Michael Woodrow and sister Meredith Lee.

I grew up between that gold-rush town and Juneau, where we moved after my father became the first commissioner of public works when Alaska became a state in 1959. That's where my younger sister, Deborah Lynn, was born in 1965 – shortly after my mother christened the *Taku*, the Alaska Marine Highway System's second ferry.

In 1973, I married and then spent 22 years in King Salmon with my fisheries biologist husband, Donald Bill. I worked for Bristol Bay Telephone Cooperative Inc. and raised two children, Kimberly and Ryan, and a foster daughter, Amie Morgan.

When the children graduated from Bristol Bay High School, and Don retired from the Alaska Department of Fish and Game, we moved to Anchorage. I went back to school in 1999, at the tender age of 48, and learned that I had a passion for writing. I earned a bachelor's degree in journalism in May 2003 from the University of Alaska

Anchorage and have spent the past few years writing my own award-winning articles for various Alaska newspapers and magazines while working on this labor of love.

Condensed versions of articles found in "Aunt Phil's Trunk" appeared in The Anchorage Chronicle, a weekly newspaper published by Alaska Newspapers Inc., from July 2002 until the paper closed its doors on Dec. 31, 2004. The Senior Voice, a monthly Alaska newspaper, picked up the column in February 2005 and it continues to appear in that publication.

I truly hope you enjoy this volume packed with Aunt Phil's articles and other stories that came from research jotted down in piles of notebooks, countless lined tablets and in the margins of rare books.

– Laurel Downing Bill

Charles, left, and Robert L. Mathison, maternal grandfather of Laurel Downing Bill, walk away from the Pacific Coast Trading Company and U.S. Mineral Surveyor and Assaying Office in Seward around 1906. The brothers, who mined with their father, Robert Burns Mathison, prospected around the gold-rush town of Hope.

TABLE OF CONTENTS

WORLD WAR II ERUPTS

1

DEFENSE FOR ALASKA

"Tora! Tora! Tora!" screamed Japanese flight commander Mitsuo Fuchida as he led 183 bombers and Zeros during an early morning attack on Pearl Harbor Dec. 7, 1941. By 8 a.m., hundreds of bombs were falling on airfields and battleships around the Hawaiian port.

The USS Shaw exploded after bombs hit their mark during the Japanese raid of Pearl Harbor Dec. 7, 1941.

The *USS Arizona* burned and sank after being attacked by Japanese bombers. It became the final resting place for 1,177 American crew members who died Dec. 7, 1941.

A second wave, with another 167 attack planes, followed an hour later and destroyed more ships and shipyards.

Within two hours, the sneak attack had killed 2,402 Americans, destroyed five battleships, put three out of commission, sank or damaged almost a dozen other warships and obliterated more than 180 aircraft on the ground.

The Japanese lost 27 planes and five midget submarines.

In addition to Pearl Harbor, Japan also attacked the U.S. territory of Guam, the Philippines, Wake Island and Midway Island the next day, as well as British interests in Malaya and Hong Kong.

On Dec. 8, U.S. President Franklin D. Roosevelt went before both houses of Congress to request a declaration of war against Japan. Following a vote, the declaration was formalized a few hours later. Britain declared war on Japan that same day.

Three days later, Germany declared war on the United States.

Strategically situated in the North Pacific, Alaska soon became a flurry of military activity.

"If we would provide an adequate defense for the United States, we must have ... Alaska to dominate the North Pacific," said U.S. Secretary of State William Seward in a speech to convince Congress of the value of buying Alaska in the mid-1860s.

The rush for gold in the Klondike in the late 1890s brought the first surge of military to the Great Land. The U.S. government built Fort Seward at Haines, Fort Liscum at Valdez, Fort Davis at Nome and Fort St. Michael, near the village of the same name at the mouth of the Yukon River. Two more installations were established along the Yukon River – Fort Egbert at Eagle and Fort Gibbon near Tanana.

The U.S. Army Signal Corps built the Washington-Alaska Military Cable and Telegraph communication system to link the military units. It strung telegraph lines across 1,497 miles of wilderness and laid 2,128 miles of submarine cable that connected Alaska with the rest of the nation. The Corps also established a 107-mile radio link between Fort St. Michael and Port Safety on the Seward Peninsula.

After the gold rush played out, the Army withdrew. It closed all its forts between 1921-1925, except Fort Seward – renamed Chilkoot Barracks.

In 1937, as Adolf Hitler was formalizing plans for expanding German dominance in Europe and the Japanese were invading China,

Chilkoot Barracks, built south of Haines in 1904, was the first permanent U.S. military installation in Alaska. Originally named Fort William H. Seward, it was renamed Chilkoot Barracks in 1922 and was the only U.S. Army post in Alaska until World War II. Deactivated in 1946, the government sold it as surplus property to 50 World War II veterans who established it as Port Chilkoot.

Soldiers of the Headquarters Battery, 1st Battalion, 250th Coast Artillery, stand at attention for an inspection in Sitka during the early 1940s.

the U.S. Navy established a small seaplane base at Sitka. It conducted several survey flights and fleet exercises in the North Pacific and Aleutian Islands.

Tension between America and Japan grew as 1940 approached.

Suffering from the Great Depression, the United States and many European countries enacted high protective tariffs that stifled Japanese exports and increased Japan's poor economic condition – which prompted its invasion of China.

Anti-western sentiment in Japan grew after President Roosevelt decided not to renew the 1911 U.S.-Japan Treaty of Commerce and Navigation in July 1939. Then the U.S. Congress passed the Export Control Act in July 1940. These two actions eliminated Japan's primary source of oil, scrap metal and other material resources needed for war.

Not only did these actions deal a severe economic blow to Japan, they also were a slap in the face to Japan's leaders, who felt America had no right to pass judgment or to interfere in their affairs.

As tensions between Japan and the United States grew, a significant military presence started building in Alaska. Construction

The U.S. Navy chose Kodiak for its principal base, Fort Greely, at the beginning of World War II because of the ice-free waters.

of naval stations at Kodiak and Dutch Harbor began, the Naval Air Station at Sitka was expanded, and work started in June 1940 on building Fort Richardson and Elmendorf Field, near Anchorage.

And although construction of Ladd Field, east of Fairbanks, began in the fall of 1938, it welcomed its first U.S. Army Air Corps troops in spring 1940. The field served as a cold weather experimental station, an air depot for repairing and testing aircraft and the principal base in Alaska for the Air Transport Command.

It also played an important part in America's lend-lease program with the Soviet Union.

Lend-Lease Program Expands

Lend-lease started out as a plan that allowed the United States to remain officially neutral during the early years of World War II while providing monetary and material assistance to Great Britain.

In March 1941, Congress approved the Lend-Lease Act, which empowered the president to give aid to friendly nations in exchange for whatever kind of compensation or benefit he thought acceptable. Aid ranged from heavy war material and munitions to industrial equipment, raw material, agricultural products and many other items.

Initially, The Union of Soviet Socialist Republics wasn't included in the group of allies that received aid because it appeared to be on the side of the Germans.

At the beginning of the war, officially deemed to be September 1939, the Soviet Union had an agreement with Germany to invade and divide Poland and several Baltic states. But following Adolf Hitler's surprise invasion of the Soviet Union in June 1941, which destroyed thousands of warplanes in the first week of fighting, the United Kingdom and the Soviet Union formed a military alliance against Germany.

In October 1941, the U.S. government, still officially neutral, formally extended lend-lease aid to the Soviets.

For months, war supplies were shipped to the U.S.S.R. via various sea routes. Aircraft traveled either by sea across the North Atlantic or by an air-sea link from Miami to South America, Africa and Iran.

Four days after the Japanese attack on Pearl Harbor on Dec. 7, 1941, Nazi Germany declared war on the United States, drawing America into a two-theater war.

Following its declaration of war, the United States and 14 of its allies signed lend-lease agreements. Between 1941-1945, the U.S. gave its allies $50 billion in military aid. In return, America benefited from reciprocal aid, such as rental of military bases on Allied soil, the pooling of resources and manpower, and the inventive genius of every Allied power toward winning the war.

Above: During World War II, Russian officers mingled with American soldiers at the Ladd Field United Service Organizations' building, seen here. Note the mounted caribou head hanging on the center wall.

Below: Airacobra Fighters, like this one seen at Ladd Field on July 9, 1944, were a favorite of Soviet pilots.

2

RUSSIA'S SECRET MISSION

Fairbanks residents began to see strangely dressed soldiers wearing high leather boots in the fall of 1942. They were greeted with "Pryvet" and "Zdrastvuite" instead of "hello" and "good morning" in the local shops.

Although shrouded in secrecy, Ladd Field, east of Fairbanks, became a hub of Soviet activity following a lend-lease agreement between Russia and the United States. American pilots were ferrying newly built aircraft north from Montana and turning them over to Soviet flight crews at Ladd for transport to the Russian front to fight Nazis.

Prior to Ladd's opening in 1940, Alaska was a vast, undefended territory. The only active military installation was the Chilkoot Barracks, located in Haines. There were no military airfields.

Soldiers stand in a chow line at Ladd Field. The Russians can be distinguished from the Americans by their uniforms and shiny black boots.

In an effort to secure better defenses for the Last Frontier, Alaska's territorial delegate to Congress, Anthony J. Dimond, tried to persuade lawmakers of the necessity of militarizing the nation's northern border in the early 1930s.

The U.S. Army Air Corps, predecessor of the U.S. Army Air Forces and later U.S. Air Force, was evaluating defense needs in Alaska at the same time. During the summer of 1934, it sent a flight of 10 B-10 bombers from Washington, D.C., to scout for possible airfield sites. The mission's leader, future five-star general and commander of the U.S. Army Air Forces Henry H. "Hap" Arnold, recommended that an air base be built at Fairbanks that could support cold weather testing and serve as a tactical supply depot.

Both military advisory boards and high-ranking officers agreed that air bases should be established in Alaska.

Brig. Gen. William "Billy" Mitchell knew Alaska firsthand through his service with the U.S. Army Signal Corps in 1901-1903. He helped scope out a portion of the route for the Washington-Alaska Military Cable and Telegraph System and believed in the capabilities of air-

Prior to World War II, Fairbanks was a quiet little town. The Alaska Railroad depot and Immaculate Conception Catholic Church steeple can be seen from this rooftop view of the Cushman Street bridge during the late 1930s.

planes. He also thought Alaska the "air crossroads of the world" and of utmost importance to America's defense.

"I believe in the future, he who holds Alaska will hold the world ...," Mitchell told Congress. "I think it is the most strategic place in the world."

The Wilcox National Air Defense Act, passed by Congress in 1935, authorized the construction of new air bases around the country. The bill included a cold weather testing and training facility for Alaska, but it did not provide funding.

Alaska's delegate to Congress, Anthony J. Dimond, urged Congress to build military facilities in the territory.

Arnold continued to pressure Congress for funds.

"Our people must be trained to fly up there, about the weather and the kind of clothing they must have. How to start an engine when it is 40 degrees below zero," he testified early in 1939. "There is going to be an awful lot to learn."

Congress finally appropriated $4 million to build the airfield, and in August 1939, surveyors arrived and got the project under way.

One month later, Germany invaded Poland. Britain, France, Australia, New Zealand, India, South Africa and Canada declared war on Germany.

The first Army Air Corps troops arrived in Fairbanks during April 1940 and dove into construction of the airfield. Maj. Dale V. Gaffney,

The first survey team, shown above, landed on an unpaved strip in Fairbanks in August 1939. From left, Cadet John Lee Jr.; Maj. Newton Longfellow; Maj. Dale V. Gaffney, later promoted to brigadier general; Col. John C. H. Lee, in command of the party; Maj. E. M. George, the constructing quartermaster in charge of the new $4 million airbase; and Capt. C. W. Gibson.

the first commander, named it Ladd Army Airfield in honor of Maj. Arthur K. Ladd, an aviator killed in a plane crash in South Carolina in 1935. Gaffney soon became a brigadier general.

By summer 1940, troops had poured a 5,000-foot concrete runway and foundations for 12 buildings and hangars.

Arnold – now Chief of the Army Air Corps – was so impressed during an inspection in September that he declared the base operational. Ladd Army Airfield was officially born, even though permanent buildings, including hangars, weren't ready.

The first two B-17 Flying Fortresses arrived at the Cold Weather Test Detachment for experimental work the next month. Soon the Detachment was testing almost every model of aircraft in the Air Corps inventory, including bombers, fighters, transports and helicopters.

And without permanent facilities in place, the mechanics worked on the airplanes "in raw wind and incredible temperatures on naked runways," according to one source.

Through all the hardships, vital lessons for operating aircraft in arctic conditions were learned at Alaska's first Army airfield. The cold weather experimental station focused on developing standards for servicing and operating planes in subzero temperatures, testing a multitude of aircraft parts and analyzing arctic operations that included communications equipment, medical issues and survival gear.

The experimental station's development of electric underwear was a big hit with aviators faced with flying un-pressurized planes in sub-arctic temperatures. Combat crews in Europe benefited, too, as the toasty undergarments kept them warm during long, cold bombing raids.

In the fall of 1942, the United States and the Soviet Union signed a lend-lease agreement that made Ladd Field a vital link in a secret mission to get American-made aircraft to the Russian front. Ladd became the official aircraft transfer point between the two nations.

Cold Weather Test Detachment personnel endured frigid temperatures at Ladd Field in Fairbanks.

The countries agreed that Americans would ferry newly manufactured airplanes from U.S. factories to an airbase in Great Falls,
Mont., where the Alaska Wing worked on any modifications needed
for the planes. Then, with Canadian approval, Americans flew the
planes along the 1,900-mile Northwest Staging Route across western
Canada through Edmonton, Fort Nelson and Whitehorse, and then
on to Interior Alaska.

The Americans wanted to fly the planes on to Siberia, but Russian
leader Joseph Stalin said no. He didn't want any appearance of U.S.-
Soviet collaboration in the Far East, as his country and Japan were
not at war and he wanted to avoid any incidents that might incite the
Japanese.

The first Soviet pilots landed at Ladd Field on Sept. 24, 1942, and
trained for five days. Following an official transfer ceremony, Russian
pilots flew the stripped-down fighter planes over the first stretch
between Fairbanks, Galena and Nome – more than 400 miles.

The first Russian military mission to Alaska arrived at Nome in September 1942. The
Russian standing between the U.S. officer in riding breeches and the Yank in the tin hat is
Col. Michael Hachin, who remained in Alaska as chief of the Russian military mission for
nearly two years.

Civilian employee Helen Roberts used an air brush to paint the Russian red star on a lend-lease aircraft at Ladd.

The distances between fuel stops were even greater in Siberia as the Russians flew on to Uel'kal, Markovo, Siemchan, Yakutsk, Kirensk, Krasnoyarsk and Novosibirsk.

Soon the program, known as the Alaska-Siberia Air Ferry Route, was in full swing and as many as 300 Russians were stationed at Ladd Field, not including the transient pilots and flight crews that rotated through from frontline duty.

The American-built airplanes typically spent about a week in the hands of Russian mechanics in Fairbanks during the summer months to get them ready to fly almost 3,500 miles to the Russian front. But during winter, it took almost a month to overhaul the planes for cold-weather duty.

The base provided the Soviets with food, sleeping quarters and hangar space.

Above: Enlisted men spent much of their time wielding axes and saws. The quantity of wood required to heat and cook at the airfields during winter was staggering. About 30 men were detailed at Watson Lake and 20 at Whitehorse specifically to chop it.

Below: Russian GI's liked "pin-ups," too.

Above: Natalie Fenelonova often interpreted for Russian mechanics.

Below: A Russian flight crew performed a final check on a Douglas A-20 Havoc attack bomber before taking off for Siberia.

When it came to flying, the Russians always led the field and were given priority for takeoff, according to Otis Hays Jr. in "The Alaska-Siberian Connection: The World War II Air Route." But the officers' mess was a different story.

"We took the first time that was most convenient to us," pilot Randy Acord later recalled, "and then the Russians would have to fit into that. Now that was the only place that we had an override on the Russians!"

Russian officers also could buy things at the Base Exchange and arrange for the use of motor vehicles with American drivers. Many of them took advantage of that benefit to power shop at Fairbanks' stores.

Unlike the Lower 48, Alaska had no rationing so the Russians could buy whatever they wanted to take home to their families.

A Fairbanks resident said she remembered one time she went to the NC Co. after a group of Russians had been there shopping and found very few items left on the store's shelves.

Russian officers became a common sight as they shopped in Fairbanks' stores.

"[The Russians] bought all the silk stockings, all the yard goods, all the women's clothes, right off. The NC Company was bare," said Irene Noyes, according to "The World War II Heritage of Ladd Field."

Between September 1942 and September 1945, American crews transferred almost 8,000 aircraft to Russian crews who flew them to the Soviet Union to be used in the war effort against Germany. Over the course of the lend-lease, 133 planes were lost before reaching Fairbanks, and another 73 planes and 140 air crew members between Fairbanks and Krasnoyarsk, according to Hays.

Despite Alaska's harsh winters, this more direct air-ferry route was preferred over the longer Miami-Iran-Moscow route. And more than any other operation, the lend-lease activities brought international recognition and fame to Ladd Airfield and to Fairbanks.

In 1961, Wilber M. Brucker, then Secretary of the Army, dedicated Ladd Field in Fairbanks as Fort Jonathan M. Wainwright to honor a World War II hero of Bataan.

But it was the construction of Elmendorf Air Field and Fort Richardson near Anchorage in 1940 that brought thousands of people north and bolstered Alaska's population.

This aircraft crash-landed on the airfield at Nome. But the plane was repaired and eventually reached the Russo-German front to fight Nazis.

Above: Brig. Gen. Dale V. Gaffney, commanding general of the Alaska Division, shakes hands with Col. N. S. Vasin, commander of the Russian Detachment in Nome, on Easter Sunday 1944.

Below: The 878th Port Company at Nenana ran barges of critical fuel down the Tanana and Yukon rivers to Galena, the site of an air transport command airfield in 1944.

3

ARMY BASE REVITALIZES ANCHORAGE

Before the military began building the original Fort Richardson in 1940, which later became Elmendorf Air Force Base, Anchorage was a typical small town.

In 1938, the city's 4,000 residents had no paved roads, no street or traffic lights and the police chief clocked speeders by using his stopwatch.

Anchorage still had a dirt-filled street along Fourth Avenue in 1938.

By 1939, Fourth Avenue had become a paved, bustling street.

"... a split second too soon between city blocks was cause for a speed trap," wrote Michael Carberry and Donna Lane in "Patterns of the Past."

The next year brought several improvements, including the paving of Fourth Avenue, a squad car for the police and chlorinated water. It also brought World War II.

When the war broke out overseas in September 1939, rumors ran rampant that the U.S. government planned to build a military base in Anchorage.

Alaska's delegate to Congress, Anthony J. Dimond, had been urging Congress to provide airfields, planes, military support and a highway to the Lower 48 since 1933. But his pleas did not succeed – until 1940.

Adolf Hitler invaded and occupied Denmark and Norway that April. The following month, Germany occupied Belgium and Holland. Then France surrendered.

Congress finally realized that Russia, at the time an ally of Germany, only lay 55 miles away from Alaska at the point where the Seward Peninsula and the Chukotka Peninsula reach out toward each other.

WORLD WAR II ERUPTS

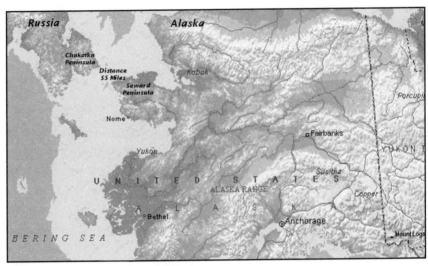

Only 55 miles separate Alaska and Russia in the Bering Sea.

The House and Senate approved the first billion-dollar budget for the U.S. Army, which included more than $12 million for an Anchorage air base.

The land for the base, about four miles north of downtown Anchorage, had been withdrawn by Presidential Order No. 8102 in April 1939. And although most of the 43,490 acres were in the public domain, some portions were homesteads that had to be purchased.

Maj. E.M. George, the Army's construction quartermaster, arrived in Anchorage from Ladd Field on June 7, 1940. He hired a few dozen local men to clear land and begin working on construction. He soon ran short of laborers.

But the then-handsome wage of .90 cents an hour ensured a steady stream of workers to the area. Within a year and a half, Anchorage would see its population explode to more than 9,000 as military personnel, construction people and civilian employees built the Army post and airfield – initially called the Anchorage Air Base.

With the population surge, housing became a major problem.

"Construction workers walked the streets at night and many spread blankets and slept on the ground," wrote Elizabeth Tower in

The first contingent of soldiers for Fort Richardson disembarked from an Alaska Railroad train on June 27, 1940. The train also brought flatbed cars loaded with U.S. Army trucks.

"Anchorage," part of the City History Series. "Families remodeled garages or built tar-paper shacks on the back of their lots and rented them at fantastic prices."

On June 27, 1940, Anchorage residents greeted a special Alaska Railroad train carrying the air base's first contingent of soldiers from the 3rd Infantry Division of Fort Lewis, Wash. The rest of the 761 men, who had all landed in Seward on board the USS St. Mihiel on June 26, arrived the next morning. The largest military force ever sent to Alaska at the time, the group included the base's first engineering company and various infantry and artillery units.

The men pitched tents on an old hay field that lay between town and the Chugach Mountains. They endured hordes of mosquitoes, miserable rainy conditions and relied on getting water from a 2-inch pipe laid to Sheep Creek.

Col. Simon Bolivar Buckner Jr. arrived in Anchorage on July 22 to assume command of the newly created Alaska Defense Force. He dove into learning about his new territory and organizing military defense for Alaska.

Above: Fort Richardson's first soldiers pitched tents in the wilderness north of Anchorage in June 1940.

Below: Spectators watched a jeep towing an anti-tank gun in the 1940 Fourth of July parade in Anchorage.

Above: Some hardy U.S. Army soldiers bathed in Ship Creek's cold waters — until locals complained about their water supply being contaminated. That problem was resolved when the soldiers were offered the use of showers at Anchorage's high school, pictured here.

Below: This aerial view shows Fort Richardson under construction on the left, looking east toward the Chugach Mountains with Knik Arm on the bottom left.

Buckner faced a monumental task, as Alaska had no airfields suitable for military aircraft and no land routes to connect it with the Continental United States. Other than Ladd Army Airfield, which was under construction, the only other Army installation in the Last Frontier was the Chilkoot Barracks in Haines.

"Chilkoot Barracks had about as much relevance to modern warfare as one of those frontier fighting posts from the days of Custer and Sitting Bull," Alaska's then-Territorial Gov. Ernest Gruening said.

Col. Simon Bolivar Buckner Jr. was promoted to brigadier general prior to the bombing of Pearl Harbor on Dec. 7, 1941.

At the time, the Haines post had 200 men armed with World War I Springfield rifles, according to U.S. Air Force records.

"We are starting from scratch, and it will be a most interesting job," Buckner told the Anchorage Chamber of Commerce, according to an article in the Anchorage Daily Times dated July 22, 1940.

Buckner, who turned down an offer for comfortable housing, lived in a canvas tent among his men until they could be moved into completed barracks.

Construction progress for a garrison of 7,000-plus men was slow. Workers encountered muskeg, a compilation of small plants, moss and roots that went down several feet. The spongy surface had to be pealed back until crews found a solid surface, like bedrock, on which to build. Equipment, in short supply, often got stuck in the muck.

And while local resources, particularly lumber, were used whenever possible, nearly all equipment, parts and food had to come by ship from the Lower 48.

Maj. Everett S. Davis and two enlisted men flew in from Ladd Field on Aug. 12. The first Air Corps personnel to arrive at the base, the men touched down in their Martin B-10B on Merrill Field. Since Elmendorf Field was under construction, their base headquarters was a one-room cabin on sled runners at Merrill, according to Air Force records. The wanigan was used for airfield operations, general storage and sleeping quarters.

By the end of October, about 2,000 laborers were working long hours seven days a week to build a runway and make barracks and headquarters buildings habitable by winter.

A Douglas OA-5 Pelican had the honor of landing first at the new Elmendorf Field on Nov. 8, 1940.

The next day, soldiers moved into their newly constructed barracks, and the Army post was named Fort Richardson – in honor of Brig. Gen. Wilds P. Richardson, the first president of the Alaska Road Commission. The airfield was named Elmendorf Air Field to honor Capt. Hugh M. Elmendorf, an Air Corps officer killed in an air accident at Wright Field, Ohio, in 1933.

During the following year, as many as 3,415 laborers worked to complete the base. But soldiers and non-commissioned officers had to be assigned to handle freight, excavate dirt and clean up because more workers were needed.

Fort Richardson was taking shape by 1941.

Following the attack on Pearl Harbor by Japan on Dec. 7, 1941, progress on the base's construction ramped up and life changed dramatically for Alaskans.

Buckner, recently promoted to brigadier general, feared the Japanese would attack Alaska and ordered blackouts.

Residents had to tape dark shades on their windows at night or paint their windows black – leaving tiny slits in the middle for sunlight to enter.

People improvised when they ran short of black paint. They dissolved phonograph records in acetone and used the mixture as a paint substitute, according to Claus M. Naske and Ludwig J. Rowinski, authors of "Anchorage, A Pictorial History."

The Japanese attack on Pearl Harbor in Hawaii Dec. 7, 1941, startled the world and electrified Alaska. Within hours, tight security, blackouts and mass military control were instituted. Rumors in the Lower 48 already had Alaska as a Japanese conquest. Newly promoted Brig. Gen. Simon Buckner's defenses flew into action. With Elmendorf Airfield as the center of operations, the 11th Air Force was alerted and moved out toward the Aleutian Chain.

Any light that escaped could signal disaster. Streetlights were turned off, and cars drove through the winter darkness with only parking lights to illuminate the way.

Trenches also were dug to protect Anchorage citizens in the event of Japanese air attacks. When sirens sounded, residents were to leave their homes and hide in the trenches.

Buckner also ordered the evacuation of all military dependents, as well as newly arrived residents. Some longtime residents left, too.

Soldiers at Fort Richardson grew proficient using radio equipment. Seen here are Pvt. Frederick Nielsen, left, and Spc. 3 Joseph Kohler.

By April 1942, Anchorage's population had dropped to about 6,000. That number included all military personnel and construction workers who lived in town, not those who lived on the base.

Construction on air bases across Alaska went into high gear, even though the local workforce dwindled due to enlistments and the draft. Some unemployed fishermen and cannery workers hired on as laborers, but more workers were needed.

The military construction projects brought opportunity for many who lived in the Lower 48, and along with military personnel, Alaska's population swelled again. At its peak, there were about 152,000 military service people in the territory.

"As fast as boats could be loaded, they steamed to Alaska jammed to busting with defense workers and supplies. Over twenty thousand construction workers migrated north in two years," wrote Jean

Potter, who was sent to Alaska in the early 1940s by Fortune magazine. "Soldiers swarmed up faster than barracks could be built to house them. The towns near bases were thronged with officers and privates from all over the States. Trucks and jeeps tore up and down the streets. The crowded bars and restaurants looked like canteens. It seemed as if Alaska were one great Army camp, with most of its population in uniform."

The construction of Fort Richardson transferred from the Army Quartermaster Corps to the Army Corps of Engineers in January 1941. Maj. Benjamin B. Talley became the resident area engineer.

At that time, both runways and aprons were cleared and the east-west runway was graded and partially paved, according to government documents.

The first Air Corps unit arrived at Elmendorf on Feb. 21, 1941, and the 18th Pursuit Squadron quickly assembled the 20 crated P-36A Hawks that arrived with them on board the USS St. Mihiel.

More Air Corps personnel and aircraft followed in late February, transported by sea and then rail to Anchorage. That brought the num-

Brig. Gen. Simon Buckner Jr. constantly pressured officials in Washington, D.C., and the U.S. Army for newer, faster, larger bombers and fighters. For the most part, his requests fell on deaf ears, since the demand for such planes was in Europe. But in February 1941, Buckner did receive 20 P-36A Hawks, like the one pictured above. By August, only nine were operational due to aircraft fatigue, accidents and the lack of replacement parts.

Above: Military air activity was transferred from Merrill Field, seen here, after the Elmendorf north/south runway construction was completed in June 1941. But the loss of military traffic didn't impact Merrill Field. In 1942, it recorded more traffic than La Guardia Field in New York.

Below: The 11th Air Force was formed at Elmendorf Air Field in early 1942. The field played a vital role as the main air logistics center and staging area during the Aleutian Campaign and later air operations against the Kurile Islands. The bombers seen here were part of the 77th Bombardier Squadron.

ber of enlisted people on the base to more than 3,900.

Although troops and aircraft bound for Fort Richardson arrived safely in Anchorage from Seward via the Alaska Railroad, military leaders became concerned about the vulnerability of the railroad route. They thought that Japanese bombs easily could put the southernmost portion of the railroad out of commission, which would eliminate the military's main supply route.

So the demands of national defense at Fort Richardson brought the approval of another major project in the spring of 1941: a railroad spur through the mountains near Whittier.

Maj. Everett S. Davis worked closely with veteran bush pilots who were training men in cold weather flight and aircraft maintenance. Brig. Gen. Simon Buckner Jr. hired Robert "Bob" Reeve, seen here fueling a ski plane, and other bush pilots to fly supplies and materials to the various military outposts. In 1941, Reeve alone flew more than 1,100 tons of equipment and 300 men from Anchorage to military sites.

MILITARY ROUTES EMERGE

4

RAILROADER TUNNELS TO WHITTIER

A uthorization to build a railroad spur through the mountains to Whittier allowed one of Anchorage's earliest settlers to carve a name for himself during World War II.

Anton Anderson engineered the project that pierced through three miles of solid granite to open the Port of Whittier to the Railbelt and to Fort Richardson, 75 miles away. The project, overseen by the U.S. Army Corps of Engineers, was initiated because of a concern that the long railroad route to Seward, particularly the Loop District with its trestles, was vulnerable to attack by Japanese bombers. Military leaders wanted to provide the Anchorage base with a safer link to a deep-water port that would protect their main supply line.

Anderson had vast experience in railroad building in the Last Frontier. He had labored as a railroader along with many hardy men who arrived by the boatloads at Resurrection Bay after the U.S. government chose Seward as the saltwater terminus for its proposed railroad in 1915. He laid tracks across tundra, foothills and mountain slopes, working shoulder to shoulder with other Scandinavian, Russian, Greek, Slovenian and Irish laborers who poured into Alaska.

On May 24, 1917, Anderson started working as an axman on a survey party for the Alaska Road Commission. That date began a long and distinguished career that led the native New Zealander into public service and earned him the title "Mr. Alaska Railroad."

Anton Anderson, seen here surveying for the Alaska Rural Rehabilitation Corp. Matanuska Colonization Project in 1935, led a full, productive life in his adopted country.

Not only did the native New Zealander have a hand in building the Alaska Railroad in the early 1900s and engineering the tunnel to Whittier during World War II, he also surveyed the townsite of Anchorage in 1915 and was active in the town's growth.

He served as location engineer for the Matanuska Valley colonization project, was active in the promotion of the Bureau of Reclamation's Eklutna hydroelectric plant, served as chairman of Anchorage Public Utilities and was elected to serve on the Anchorage City Council. He became the city's 22nd mayor in 1956.

The railroad man resigned as mayor due to ill health late in 1958. He was honored by the Greater Anchorage Chamber of Commerce, which presented him with an honorary life membership in that group following his resignation.

"The Anchorage area is a better place to live because Anton chose to come our way," said the Alaska Railroad's then-Gen. Mgr. Robert Anderson.

Anton Anderson died in 1961 after a long battle with Parkinson's disease.

Anderson, who sought out routes for the Iron Horse to steam into the interior of Alaska, eventually became chief engineer. Through his work, he was instrumental in the development of Western Alaska and surveyed and engineered much of the railroad line.

But the feat he considered his greatest achievement was the construction of the Whittier railroad tunnel.

As early as 1902, the deep-water port on the northeast shore of the Kenai Peninsula – at the head of Passage Canal – was considered a possible entrance to the region. But John E. Ballaine, then head of the Alaska Central Railroad, nixed the idea of linking the Passage Canal and Turnagain Arm due to the cost of tunneling through Maynard Mountain. There also was concern that the glacier, named for American poet John Greenleaf Whittier in 1915, might advance and cause operational problems at the port.

The Alaska Engineering Commission also considered Whittier as the terminus for the Alaska Railroad project in 1914, as it would cut about 50 miles of track off the line. But the idea again was rejected.

World War II changed opinions.

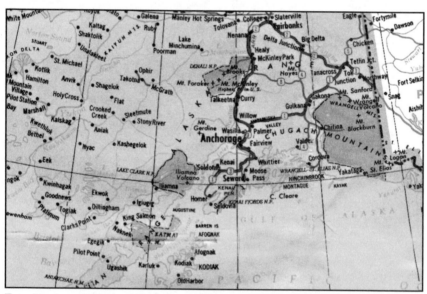

Tunneling through Maynard Mountain to Whittier, and bypassing Seward, cut the distance between Fort Richardson in Anchorage and a deep-water supply port.

The U.S. Army Corps of Engineers contracted with West Construction Co. of Boston to build two tunnels, seen here, which were known as secret destination "X-12."

The military needed a secure transportation system for troops, equipment and supplies, and a War Department study in 1940 concluded that the Passage Canal line would be safer from enemy attack than the Seward line. President Franklin D. Roosevelt approved the spur to Whittier in April 1941.

Workers drilled from both ends of the mountain, part of the

Above: Once trains began rumbling through the Anton Anderson Tunnel in 1943, military equipment and supplies were barged to the Port of Whittier, seen here, for transport to Fort Richardson and other Alaska bases.

Below: The railroad roundhouse and tracks at Whittier were a hub of military activity during World War II.

Chugach Range, toward each other. In November 1942, the two crews met in the middle.

An article that appeared in The Greatlander Shopping News on Nov. 22, 1978, told of the event.

"Anderson was at the end of one of the shafts, deep in the mountain, when the holing through was about to occur," the article reported. "Under pounding of air hammers, rocks gave way and through a small hole at his feet, Anderson could shout through to the drilling crew on the other side.

"'Where'd it come through?' he yelled.

"Back came a muffled reply, 'It's up by our heads!'

"Anderson was stunned. What had happened to his careful surveys, the figures determined by triangulation over the tops of a high mountain?"

The two shafts actually were off by about six inches, an unusual degree of accuracy for such a difficult undertaking.

The drilling crew had a good laugh at the joke they played on Anderson.

By June 1943, workers completed laying track over the 14-mile route and the first trains rolled through the Anton Anderson Tunnel into Whittier.

While Anderson and his team were burrowing through the mountain near Whittier, another team was hacking its way through rugged wilderness to link Alaska with a land route to the Lower 48.

The Alaska pioneer road from Canada to Alaska started at Dawson Creek and then headed north to Fort St. John, Fort Nelson, Watson Lake, Whitehorse, Dawson City, Tok and then ended at Delta Junction. Construction of the primitive road, originally called the Alaska-Canada Highway, began in April 1942 and ended less than nine months later at a cost of $140 million.

Workers started building the Haines Junction cutoff, authorized in November 1942, while the pioneer road was being finished. It cost more than $13 million and was completed in December 1943.

The cutoff linked the port at Haines to the Alcan Highway at Haines Junction, 160 miles away. This route allowed travel if the White Pass and Yukon Railway was blocked, provided shipment of supplies from the port to points along the highway and was a viable evacuation route out of Alaska if the enemy invaded the mainland.

MILITARY ROUTES EMERGE

5

ROAD HEADS NORTH TO ALASKA

W hile thousands of American troops fought Nazis and kamikazes in 1942, more than 10,000 U.S. soldiers battled mosquitoes, muskeg and permafrost to build a primitive road to Alaska.

Called one of America's greatest construction projects, the Alaska-Canada Highway stretched 1,422 miles from Dawson Creek, British Columbia, to Delta Junction, Alaska.

Thousands of American troops blazed a route through dense forests in the northern wilderness to connect Alaska to the Lower 48 during World War II.

Years before the military felt the need for a supply route through the vast wilderness, Edward H. Harriman proposed building a road from Chicago to the Bering Sea. In 1899, the veteran railroad man thought it would be a good idea to connect the gold fields of Alaska and Canada with the Continental United States. But when the gold fields played out, so did his idea.

It resurfaced in the 1920s.

Donald MacDonald, a locating engineer with the Alaska Road Commission, had dreamed for years of an overland coastal route to Alaska. It would run north from Seattle across British Columbia through the Yukon Territory to Fairbanks.

MacDonald and a group of Fairbanks residents formed International Highway Association Inc. to sponsor the building of such a road. Citizens of Alaska and Canada lobbied for years without success.

In the early 1930s, MacDonald heard about a Copper Center man who had boasted that he and his dog team could make it to Chicago over prospector trails. So MacDonald contacted Clyde "Slim" Williams and convinced the 50-year-old trapper to prove it.

Clyde "Slim" Williams heads down a wilderness trail in Alaska with his part-wolf dogs during the 1930s.

MILITARY ROUTES EMERGE

Clyde "Slim" Williams modified his sled with Model-T wheels to mush to the Chicago World's Fair in 1933.

With the financial backing of MacDonald and the Automobile Highway Association, Williams left Fairbanks with a team of part-wolf dogs in November 1932. Following crude maps drawn by MacDonald, he and his dog team trekked through the wilderness and made their way along MacDonald's coastal route.

They reached the existing North American Highway System in British Columbia in five months.

Williams then rigged his sled with Model-T wheels and headed east 2,000 miles to the Chicago World's Fair, where he and his dogs were a big attraction.

When the fair ended in October 1933, Williams and his dog team mushed on to Washington, D.C., where they camped in a city park and met with Alaska's Delegate, Anthony J. Dimond, and other members of Congress. He also briefed President Franklin D. Roosevelt on the proposal for a road.

Years later, Eleanor Roosevelt would say that Williams was a most vocal advocate for the Alaska Highway.

Soon after Williams' visit to the nation's capitol, Dimond introduced a bill into Congress for a highway. He found no support.

But in 1938, Roosevelt appointed the Alaska International Highway Commission to make a study of routes through the northwest.

First Lady Eleanor Roosevelt visited with adventurer and Alaska Highway advocate Clyde "Slim" Williams during his trip to the Lower 48 in 1933.

The commission submitted a favorable report and surveyed several routes, including Route A, MacDonald's coastal route. It started at Prince George and traveled through Atlin, Whitehorse and along the Tanana Valley to Fairbanks. Route B, which also started at Prince George, traveled up the Rocky Mountain Trench to Watson Lake, then on to Dawson City, down the Yukon River and connected to Fairbanks.

But plans for a highway again were tabled due to high construction costs and concern over what impacts a roadway might have on the people of the northern territories.

Williams again made a trip south in 1939 to gain support for the highway. He and adventurer John Logan, along with Siberian husky Blizzard, left Fairbanks on May 14 on board specially modified British-made motorcycles.

"We chose small, single-engine machines because we knew we

would be pushing, pulling and rafting with them," Logan later recalled.

They also welded plates on the bottoms of the cycles and added hand brakes so they could have some control while walking the machines with the engines running.

With extra gas cans strapped to the back racks, the men headed down the same route Williams had traveled a few years earlier. They jolted their way through Big Delta, Chicken, Dawson and Whitehorse.

Clyde "Slim" Williams, left, and John Logan, with their dog Blizzard, were the first to motor through the wilderness from Alaska to Seattle.

They followed pack trails, forded streams and muscled through muskeg to cover 2,300 miles in 6-1/2 months. Williams later said that he and Logan never missed a meal – but sometimes they got a few meals behind.

The team arrived in Seattle in early December. They were introduced at a Chamber of Commerce meeting as the first men to motor across the proposed Alaska International Highway.

Their journey again raised the idea of carving a road to Alaska, but the bombing of Pearl Harbor by the Japanese on Dec. 7, 1941, made building that road a reality.

Following the attack, American officials realized that Alaska was vulnerable to Japanese invasion – especially with only 750 miles separating the last island in the Aleutian Chain and the nearest Japanese military base.

Although America had purchased Alaska from Russia in 1867, the military had set up few defenses in its new territory, which is one-fifth the size of the United States. The single military base in the Aleutians, at Dutch Harbor, only had six functional aircraft and a small radio station run by the U.S. Army Signal Corps.

A U.S. Coast Guard Grumman JF-2 floatplane takes off from the water at Dutch Harbor in 1938.

Military officials decided to begin construction of the Alaska-Canada Highway at Dawson Creek, seen here in the late 1930s.

The need for more military in Alaska became urgent, and a road to transport troops, equipment and supplies became a priority.

Officials, led by Brig. Gen. C.L. Sturdevant, quickly studied their options. The Americans preferred Route A, while the Canadians favored Route B.

But Route C turned out to be the only practical plan. Also known as the Prairie Route, it started at Dawson Creek and went east of the trail Williams blazed in 1933. The route was far enough inland to avoid enemy attacks by sea, connected air bases along the Northwest Staging Route from Edmonton to Fairbanks, and traversed through relatively level land – never ascending a pass more then 4,250 feet – ending at Delta Junction on the Richardson Highway, just 98 miles east of Fairbanks.

In February 1942, President Roosevelt authorized the U.S. Army Corps of Engineers to proceed with the project.

Canada agreed to provide rights of way, waive import duties and taxes, and allow the use of timber, gravel fill and rock along the route. The United States agreed to pay for construction and maintenance of the highway for the duration of the war. The Americans also agreed to turn over the Canadian portion of the road and facilities to Canada six months after the war ended.

The first train carrying American troops arrived at Dawson Creek on March 2, 1942. They were to lay 1,200 miles of primitive road through Canada and more than 200 miles through Alaska in record time.

Dozens of private contractors, chosen by the Public Roads Administration, hired as many as 6,000 civilian workers to follow behind the troops and turn the pioneer road into a permanent highway.

Initial command of the construction project, first called the Alaska-Canada Military Highway, was handed to Gen. William M. Hoge. He designated Fort St. John as the southern headquarters and Whitehorse the northern headquarters. But due to the size of the project, later dubbed the Alcan, Col. James A. O'Connor soon took over the southern sector.

The first four regiments sent north split up and began building parts of the rough military road toward each other. The 35th Combat Engineers proceeded from Dawson Creek to Fort Nelson; the 340th General Service Regiment built from Whitehorse south; the 341st General Service Regiment worked from Fort St. John to Fort Nelson; and the 18th Combat Engineer Regiment went to Skagway, then traveled by train to Whitehorse to build the road northwest toward Alaska.

Trains soon delivered troops and supplies to Dawson Creek and Whitehorse.

These five men were part of a group of 3,000-plus African-American soldiers who took part in building the Canadian portion of the Alaska-Canada Highway.

Bush pilots spent countless hours flying Army and Public Road Administration engineers around to check the terrain. Canadians also helped by scouting trails and finding the best possible ground on which to build the road and where to cross the rivers.

Short of men, another three engineering regiments were added: the 93rd, 95th and 97th. These regiments, made up of African-American soldiers with white officers, changed perceptions of the time.

Many in the military thought black engineers were not as skilled and industrious as Caucasians. At a time when segregation and Jim Crow laws were commonplace, using white and black troops on the same project was seen as experimental.

African-American and white units had been kept separate since the Civil War. Black soldiers were considered "careless, shiftless, irresponsible and secretive," according to a report commissioned by the Army War College.

They were assigned mostly to labor-intensive service positions and often issued less equipment and fewer supplies than their white counterparts.

In one case, while building the Alaska-Canada Highway, the 95th Engineer Regiment had no bulldozers or other machinery to clear trees because the equipment was given to the less experienced all-white 35th Regiment, according to a Public Broadcasting System article. The African-Americans had to make do with shovels, picks, handsaws and wheelbarrows.

But the black troops sent to build the highway changed many people's minds. The hard-working men worked shoulder to shoulder to help build hundreds of miles of road through densely forested land in just eight months. Their contribution to the road effort helped change the situation for African-Americans in the military – which desegregated in 1948.

All the troops worked through temperatures exceeding 50 degrees below zero during the winter months. Many were from warm climates, such as California, Florida and the Deep South, and working in such conditions came as quite a shock.

Soldiers endured bitter temperatures when they arrived to work on the Alaska-Canada Highway.

Soldiers were issued heavy parkas, thick fur hats and mittens, and double sets of long underwear. They had pyramidal tents that slept six. The men also received two heavy down-filled sleeping bags each, which they tucked one inside the other and crawled in fully clothed.

In June, they suffered through constant rain that turned the sodden ground into a quagmire that grabbed vehicles and held them by the hubcaps. They then labored night and day during the summer, when the sun provided more than 20 hours of light and temperatures rose to 90 degrees above zero.

Surveyors first mapped the route, working about 10 miles ahead of men using heavy equipment. They followed existing winter roads, old Indian trails and rivers. Sometimes routing of the road relied on "sight engineering." Other soldiers followed close behind to blaze the trail, and a battalion of bulldozers then knocked down trees in a path roughly 50 to 90 feet across. A second battalion brought up the rear, quickly flattening the road surface.

The routine was the same day after day as the troops hacked their way through spruce, jack pine and aspen trees.

"There ain't nothin' but miles and miles of nothin' but miles and miles," one soldier said.

Above: U.S. Army Corps of Engineer surveyors stayed about 10 miles ahead of bulldozers as they mapped the rough route.

Below: Soldiers followed the surveyors and axed their way through dense forests.

Above: A regiment manning bulldozers followed the axmen and plowed down more trees and flattened stumps.

Below: Another group traveled after the bulldozers to widen and level the road.

When the soldiers came across muskeg and permafrost, they used a process called corduroying to make suitable surfaces for vehicle traffic. As shown above, logs are laid close together so fill can be placed on top.

Speed was of the essence. If the men couldn't go through an obstacle, they went over it.

Early on they encountered seas of mud and muskeg and learned that the only way to get across these soggy swamps was to corduroy the road.

The men chopped down trees, layered the logs across the decaying vegetation and then poured fill over the logs. This time-consuming process slowed progress. In two months, the troops had built only 95 miles of road.

Writer Froelich Rainey traveled on the highway while it was under construction.

"We were six hours traveling less than 15 miles," he wrote in an article for the National Geographic magazine in 1943, "and everyone was wet and plastered with mud from head to toe."

After the Japanese bombed Dutch Harbor on June 3, 1942, and then seized Attu and Kiska islands, the crews picked up their pace. Many thought the Japanese were invading all of Alaska.

Many pieces of equipment became stuck in the muck.

"Every Saturday and Sunday we had a brush fire somewhere that we had to go out and put out," recalled John Bollin, a worker on the Alaska Highway. "The propaganda was the Japs were setting off fire balloons to deter what we was doing."

In July, engineer troops and civilians joined forces. Civilian contractors stopped working on improvements and instead moved up and down the line to speed up the pioneer road construction. It was a race of men and machines against the coming cold weather. If a vehicle broke down, it was pushed over the side. Nothing stopped construction.

By the beginning of September, the workers had fought dust clouds, mosquitoes and high temperatures to complete almost 1,000 miles of road.

"You had mosquitoes that dive-bombed you," engineer Hayward Oubre later recalled. "They'd dive like the Japanese with the dive-bombing. ..."

MILITARY ROUTES EMERGE

Troops, supplies and equipment to build the Alaska-Canada Highway arrived by horse, riverboat, train and plane.

Construction workers lived in temporary camps because they moved every two to three days. Note the mess tent in the middle.

Right: Road signs showing the way home reminded soldiers of the lives they left behind.

Below: Daring soldiers often befriended bears along the construction route.

Above: Building bridges across streams, creeks and rivers was a tough job.

Below: On large crossings, soldiers built temporary bridges on pontoons and then forded the waterway with a permanent log structure.

MILITARY ROUTES EMERGE

The engineers spent a lot of time near water, building more than 130 bridges. Several lost their lives during the construction. The worst accident occurred at Charlie Lake, when 17 soldiers were dumped off a raft into the frigid waters. Only five survived.

Above: Before the Alaska-Canada Highway project got under way, the Richardson Highway between Valdez and Fairbanks was a rough, wilderness road.

Below: The U.S. Corps of Engineers upgraded the Richardson Highway between Delta Junction and Fairbanks.

Soldiers building the rough trail to Alaska had to work in freezing temperatures.

Workers only had 460 miles left to build before winter set in when they ran into a long stretch of permafrost along the west side of Kluane Lake that stopped construction for six weeks, according to "The Trail of '42," written by Stan Cohen. None of the engineers had experience with building on semi-frozen ground that can thaw and turn into mud with a temperature change of a few degrees.

Permafrost lurked beneath seemingly solid ground. When bulldozers stripped away the protective layers of topsoil and vegetation, the frozen ground melted.

"You got a canal of mud," Walter Mason, a lieutenant with the 97th, later said.

The builders finally resorted to insulating the permafrost by corduroying on top of it, which got the project under way again.

Fall brought one of the coldest autumns on record. Men constantly checked each other for white spots on their skin – an indication of frostbite.

The last portion of the Alaska-Canada Highway was completed on Oct. 25, 1942, when a crew working south from Alaska met a crew coming north from Whitehorse and they closed the southern section of the road at Beaver Creek.

Canadian Minister of Pensions and National Health Ian MacKenzie and acting Alaska Gov. E.L. "Bob" Bartlett cut the ribbon on Nov. 20, 1942, to officially open the military road.

A ceremony on Nov. 20 at Soldiers' Summit, overlooking Kluane Lake, officially marked the completion of the highway and opened it to military traffic. In temperatures hovering around 30 degrees below zero, Canadian Minister of Pensions and National Health Ian MacKenzie spoke to the men gathered.

"I desire to express the admiration of the government of Canada to the American Corps of Engineers for one of the greatest engineering marvels in the whole world. Carry on that splendid work," he said. "This road is built for war, but this road will be used when peace and victory come back to us again. This road will again be used for the great purposes of reconstruction and of peace."

Built in less than nine months, the rough trail and its 133 bridges were a great accomplishment, but it was not finished. Many of the

U.S. military vehicles soon were traveling the new Alaska-Canada Highway.

bridges washed out the next spring and had to be repaired or rebuilt. The Public Roads Administration continued improving and straightening the road for the next several years.

The United States turned over the Canadian portion of the highway to the Canadian government in April 1946, and the highway was opened to civilian traffic late in 1948.

But it was nearly impassible for anything other than trucks and bulldozers. For years it was a muddy, single-lane road that climbed steep hills and had many dangerous curves. Travelers had to carry adequate fuel, food and emergency gear as there were few facilities.

Construction of the 150-mile Glenn Highway that connected Palmer to the Richardson Highway and the rest of Alaska, Canada and the Lower 48, began in 1941. Although it was opened to military traffic in October 1942, it wasn't completed until 1945.

The route traveled through Glennallen, a camp on the Richardson Highway in the Copper River Valley. It was named after two U.S. Army explorers of the late 1800s: Capt. Edwin Glenn and Lt. Henry T. Allen.

This sign near Glennallen indicated that drivers might not experience perfect driving conditions on the Glenn Highway.

6

Outposts Sprout Up

I n 1940, the U.S. military rapidly built up Alaska's defenses. Along with Ladd Field in Fairbanks and Fort Richardson in Anchorage, construction of U.S. Navy stations at Kodiak and Dutch Harbor began.

The naval base at Sitka also expanded so PBY Catalina flying boats could patrol the Gulf of Alaska and the length of the Aleutian Islands.

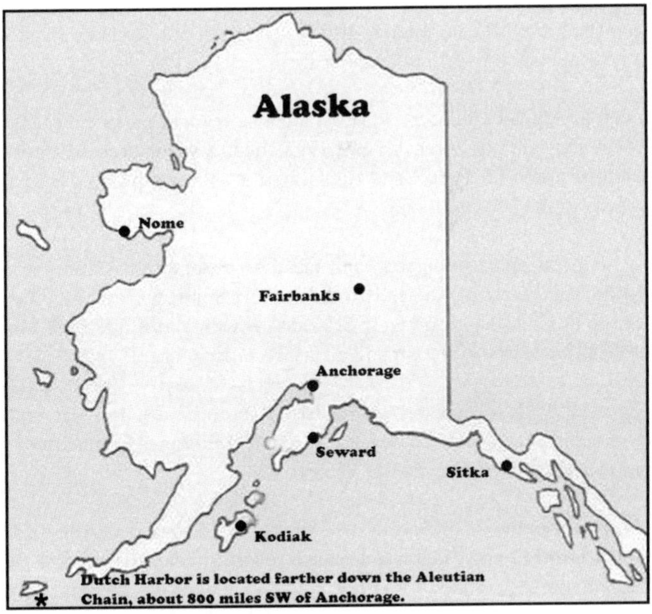

The U.S. Army Coast Artillery Corps took charge of defending the three U.S. Navy air stations at Kodiak, Dutch Harbor and Sitka, as well as the strategic port of Seward.

Alaska

Nome

Fairbanks

Anchorage

Seward

Sitka

Kodiak

Dutch Harbor is located farther down the Aleutian Chain, about 800 miles SW of Anchorage.

Kodiak

The road above led to Fort Greely on Kodiak during World War II.

Kodiak became a major staging area for North Pacific operations during the war. The population of the tiny village soared to more than 25,000.

Construction of the U.S. Navy Base in Kodiak began in 1939. Its joint operations center directed Alaska operations during 1942-1943. The principal advance naval base in Alaska and the North Pacific when World War II broke out, Kodiak's ships and submarines played a critical role in the Aleutian campaign.

Fort Greely, with its coast artillery and infantry troops, stood ready to repel invaders, but the enemy did not come. In April 1943, the U.S. Army erected a permanent eight-inch gun battery north of Kodiak and established it as a sub-post of Fort Greely, naming it Fort Abercrombie.

A radio range, radar beacon and weather observation station were placed on Chirikof Island, southwest of Kodiak Island. And Fort Smith, a temporary Army housing camp, was set up at Chiniak – southwest of Kodiak – with about 500 men. The fort had an auxiliary airfield, air warning system and a surface radar unit.

Cape Greville, located on Kodiak Island south of Chiniak, was commissioned as a radio and radar beacon station in April 1943. And Entrance Point, also on the island, served as an anti-aircraft training center early in 1942.

Afognak, northeast of Kodiak on Afognak Island, was established as an administrative site in March 1942 and used as a dispersal point for seaplanes in case of a raid on Kodiak and a pilot training station.

Afognak Island, near Kodiak, also was used as a recreational site because it provided excellent trout and salmon fishing. It offered superb bear hunting opportunities, too, as seen in this photograph of Maj. Marvin "Muktuk" Marston holding the head of a 1,800-pound Kodiak brown bear shot there.

Dutch Harbor

Above: Dutch Harbor Naval Operating Base and Fort Mears, seen here, were two U.S. military installations built next to each other on Unalaska Island in response to the growing war threat with Japan. A 1938 U.S. Navy board recommended the construction, which began in July 1940. The first U.S. Army troops arrived in June 1941, and the Navy air base was finished in September. At the time of the Japanese attack on the Aleutian Islands in June 1942, these two bases had about 6,000 troops assigned.

Below: U.S. soldiers maintained their sense of humor in Dutch Harbor, as shown by this staging of dummies Charlie McCarthy and Mortimer Snerd ready for combat.

Sitka

In 1937, the U.S. Navy secured a small appropriation to establish facilities at Sitka for servicing its PBY Catalinas. A year later, a naval board urged the construction of a naval air station at Sitka, as well as stations at Kodiak and Dutch Harbor. Congress appropriated funds in 1939 and the Navy employed a civilian contractor, Siems Drake Puget Sound, to begin construction.

The Navy formally commissioned the Sitka Naval Air Station on Oct. 1, 1939, the first such installation in Alaska to become operational. Operations on Japonski Island soon expanded to include a radio station, naval section base, U.S. Marine barracks and subordinate naval shore activities. Although the scope of its operations did not grow as large as those at Kodiak and Dutch Harbor, Sitka was re-designated as a naval operating base on July 20, 1942, and supported 30,000 troops.

Soldiers built a dock at Fort Babcock, located at Shoals Point on the south end of Kruzof Island, at the base of the dormant Mt. Edgecumbe volcano near Sitka. The fort included a coastal defense gun battery, watchtower, searchlights and other supporting facilities. It was under construction from 1941 to 1944, when it was no longer needed. The six-inch guns were never installed, and the roads, bunkers and buildings were abandoned.

Fort Ray is the name most often applied to all military installations in Sitka. It began as the barracks and other structures on Charcoal and Alice islands in 1941, and was the U.S. Army's headquarters at Sitka from 1941.

The Army harbor defenses of Sitka were quite extensive. The Army constructed three modern six-inch gun batteries, a battery with two six-inch U.S. Navy guns, and a 155 mm battery surrounding the entrance to Sitka Sound. The Army also built two 90 mm anti-motor torpedo boat gun batteries for protection of the inner islands of Sitka Sound, according to National Historical Park records. These large-gun batteries each required many support facilities, including searchlights, targeting stations and radar facilities on many islands in Sitka Sound and surrounding waters.

In 1943, Makhnati Island – including the causeway and the Sitka naval operating base on Japonski Island – was declared the headquarters post of the harbor defenses of Sitka and named Fort Rousseau, in honor of Maj. Gen. Lowell H. Rousseau.

Fort Pierce included Biorka Island and several smaller islands nearby and was composed of coastal defense artillery, radar antennas, searchlights, fire-control stations, radio stations and other supporting facilities. The six-inch gun battery was abandoned just before it became operational, along with the central traverse magazine between gun positions.

Above: About 30,000 military personnel, like those above, came from all over the United States to Sitka, which created boomtown conditions. As one longtime resident watched boatloads of troops cross Sitka Sound, he said "old Alaska" was lost. "...This is about as bad as being invaded by the enemy."

Below: Some soldiers managed to enjoy themselves during quiet moments, as evidenced by these men playing baseball at Fort Rousseau on Makhnati Island.

Other Military Activity

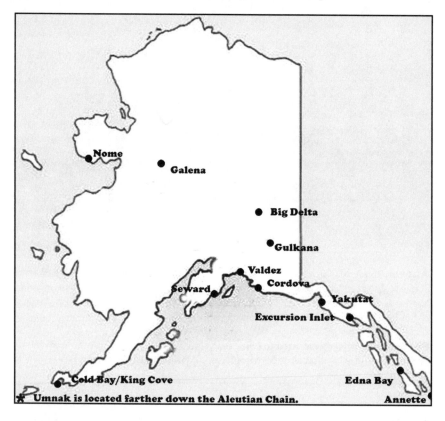

In addition to Fairbanks, Anchorage, Kodiak, Dutch Harbor and Sitka, many other U.S. military airfields, bases and various facilities popped up around Alaska between 1940 and 1944. The map above shows the locations of several such sites.

Annette Island

Annette Island saw a flurry of military activity during World War II – mostly Canadian.

In August 1940, a 20-man Civilian Conservation Corps crew from Ketchikan prepared quarters on Annette for an advance group of U.S. Army Corps of Engineers who were to build an airfield there.

The Army engineers continued work on the field through the winter of 1941-42, under the command of Maj. George J. Nold.

Canada offered to man the field and had its No. 115 Fighter Squadron in place by May 5, 1942. It was the first Canadian force ever based in a U.S. territory to directly assist in American defense.

Soon Canadian soldiers, like those pictured above, were a common site strolling on the wooden sidewalks of the base and in the little community of Metlakatla. From left, a Canadian officer from the Royal Canadian Air Force; Cmdr. Paul F. Foster; Lt. Cmdr. William Miller Jr.; U.S. Army officer (commanding officer at Annette) and Lt. Cmdr. James S. Russell.

Big Delta

Big Delta Army Airfield, established in 1942, was named for the delta formed by the confluence of the Delta and Tanana rivers about 100 miles south of Fairbanks. It later was renamed Allen Army Airfield.

In 1928, a herd of 23 bison were brought from the National Bison Range in Montana to an area south of Big Delta.

The huge animals sometimes made landings dangerous at the airfield.

Cordova

The U.S. Navy had a radio station near Cordova at Mile 7 along the Copper River and Northwestern Railroad.

Cold Bay

Above: The U.S. Navy set up an air field station at Cold Bay, located near the end of the Alaska Peninsula, commissioned July 14, 1942. The U.S. Army built Fort Randall and manned it with about 2,500 troops.

Below: The military laid cable in Cold Bay for its communication system. A radio range, radar beacon and weather observation station were established at Sanak, on Canton Island, south of Cold Bay.

Edna Bay

Above: As big guns guarded Southeast Alaska's shores, huge log rafts were gently coaxed out of Edna Bay bound for Washington state. World War II had created a demand for high-quality spruce to construct fighter planes.

The Alaska Spruce Log Program, established in 1942, brought 200 people to the headquarters at Edna Bay, west of Prince of Wales Island. Since the goal was to harvest 100 million board feet of spruce annually, nine logging camps went to work cutting the timber.

Cut logs were formed into Davis rafts – oceangoing log rafts measuring 280 feet long by 60 feet wide by 30 feet deep. Tugboats towed the enormous rafts to mills in Puget Sound.

Below: A logger stands on a springboard as he cuts his way through a giant spruce tree at Edna Bay. The program ended in 1944 when metal replaced wood in the fighter planes.

Excursion Inlet

Sounds of saws bringing down trees and roars of B-29 bombers landing on a primitive runway shattered the usual silence of the wilderness around Gustavus soon after the Japanese attacked Dutch Harbor in June 1942.

That August, the U.S. Army brought World War II to the area's homesteaders as it built a huge, secret supply terminal where giant Sitka spruce once stood.

The terminal at Excursion Inlet, just east of the monument boundary with Canada on the west coast of Lynn Canal in Southeast Alaska, covered about 600 acres and had more than 800 buildings and three docks.

But by the time the facility was completed in November 1943, the main theater of war had moved away from Alaska so the terminal was used only for a few months.

In June 1945, the military brought 700 German prisoners of war north to dismantle the huge facility. Some of the salvaged material was used to help rebuild the village of Hoonah, which had been devastated by fire in June 1944.

The photograph above shows dozens of German POWs returning to the stockade.

Above: The huge mess hall at the secret Excursion Inlet terminal fed hundreds of German POWs.

Below: The German POWs had comfortable lodgings at Excursion Inlet.

MILITARY ROUTES EMERGE

Galena

Baker Engineers employees surveyed property adjacent to the civilian runway at the U.S. Army air base in Galena.

The engineering company was under contract with the Army Air Forces to build a runway for a military airfield in 1944-1945.

Gulkana

A military runway was built at Gulkana, seen here during the 1930s, to aid the war effort.

Nome

This panoramic view of the U.S. Army air base at Nome from the hills 25 miles away shows the runway divided the tents-only area on the near side from the tent and Quonset hut mix on the far side. Two fuel trucks can be seen parked just above the runway where nearly 8,000 aircraft landed on their way through Mark Army Air Field headed to Russia during the lend-lease program between 1942 and 1944.

Seward

Many buildings in 1942 Seward, as well as the Standard Oil storage tanks, were painted as part of the World War II camouflage effort.

Above: Care was taken to camouflage structures, like the Balto building at the Jesse Lee Home complex in Seward, so the enemy couldn't see them from the air.

Below: Fort Raymond in Seward, on the southern portion of the Kenai Peninsula, was a vast tent camp spread out on the flats in front of the Jesse Lee Home. The U.S. Army Corps of Engineers built the camp, which was commissioned July 31, 1942, and had a defense garrison of about 5,000 troops. It became a naval auxiliary air facility.

Umnak

In 1941-42, Brig. Gen. Simon Bolivar Buckner Jr. built a secret base on the third-biggest island of the Aleutian Chain. Without authorization from his superiors, he stockpiled as many construction supplies as he could from other projects and sent them to the "Blair Fish Packing Co.," an outfit whose real intention was to build a U. S. Army Air Forces base on the island of Umnak.

Those who knew the island had serious doubts that a 3,000- by 100-foot runway could be constructed there, as the mountainous land mass of around 675 square miles had no natural harbors or trees.

Buckner solved the problem by importing three million square feet of Marsden Matting, seen above, which is a perforated-steel plating that can be assembled with other steel plates to create a flat surface upon which aircraft can take off and land.

In November 1941, Buckner finally received authorization to build an airfield on the island. By April 1942, the airfield was usable. And within two months, it had a garrison of 4,000 troops.

While stationed at Fort Glenn on Umnak Island, Col. William O. Eareckson of the 11th Provisional Bombing Command, who received the Distinguished Service Cross, wrote a message on a bomb destined for Japanese soldiers on the island of Kiska in 1942.

Valdez

Above: The American flag flies high over the U.S. Army Signal Corps office in Valdez.

Below: A serviceman stands on top of the wings of a U.S. Navy scout plane from the *USS Louisville* near Valdez.

Yakutat

A Douglas B-18 Bolo from the 73rd Bomber Squadron, the first bomber to use the new facility at Yakutat, taxis up the landing strip.

The 406th Bombardment Squadron was garrisoned at Yakutat Army Air Field.

Both Royal Canadian Air Force officers and U.S. Navy personnel can be seen in this photograph as the men look at bombers on the Yakutat field.

A FEW GOOD MEN

7

ESKIMO SCOUTS VOLUNTEER

When the U.S. Government needed them, Alaska's Native people came out in droves. From the beaches of Bristol Bay to the far corners of Bethel, Kotzebue, Unalakleet and Barrow, villagers didn't hesitate to provide Alaska with a line of defense after the Japanese bombed Pearl Harbor on Dec. 7, 1941.

Families, like this one from Unalakleet, were eager to volunteer for the Alaska Territorial Guard.

U.S. Army Maj. Marvin R. Marston conceived the idea of an Alaska Native defense force after visiting St. Lawrence Island on a military moral-boosting trip with comedian Joe E. Brown.

While on the island, Marston noted that all the white men, except for a school teacher, had left and that the 700 Natives living in the island's two villages of Savoonga and Gambell were nervous about possible occupation by Japanese forces.

After Marston learned that a crew from a Japanese vessel had recently come ashore and spent several days on the island, he thought about setting up defense units comprised of Alaska Natives throughout western Alaska.

His military superiors found no merit in his idea, but Marston did find staunch support from Alaska Territorial Gov. Ernest Gruening, who also wanted to set up a local guard.

Gruening had organized the first National Guard in Alaska soon after he took office on Dec. 5, 1939. Although he requested five companies be authorized in Ketchikan, Juneau, Anchorage, Fairbanks and Nome, the federal authorities only authorized the first four.

But following the bombing of Pearl Harbor, the Alaska National Guard was federalized and became the 297th Infantry. Other available men had been drafted overseas. That left the 586,000-square-mile territory, whose military bases were still under construction, woefully unprotected.

Territorial Gov. Ernest Gruening, seen here, supported an Alaska Territorial Guard to watch over Alaska during World War II.

"... I determined that every able-bodied male otherwise not in military or essential-to-war service would be enrolled in a territorial guard and kept at home for our defense if needed," Gruening wrote in his introduction to Marston's book, "Men of the Tundra."

The governor authorized the Alaska Territorial Guard and put Marston and Capt. Carl Scheibner of the Alaska Command in charge of recruitment. And early in 1942, Gruening flew with Marston to the Kuskokwim area.

Gruening didn't know what to expect from the Native people. He had little firsthand experience with them but had read how they had been affected negatively by the intrusion of white men into their land – including depletion of their food supply, decimation by diseases and taken advantage of due to their naiveté.

"I wondered whether deep-seated resentments might not lurk behind their outwardly friendly appearances," he later said. "My doubts were soon set at rest. Everywhere I found only the heartiest response to my pleas for organization in self-defense."

Gruening also noted that the response of the white men and Native men differed when asked to join the territorial guard.

Company D 1st Scout Battalion Alaska National Guard passes in review during a parade at Camp Denali on Fort Richardson near Anchorage during the early 1940s.

A FEW GOOD MEN

U.S. Army Maj. Marvin Marston mingled easily with Alaska's Native people. He's seen here, front left, at a gathering sitting on caribou skins.

"In various communities white men asked how much they would be paid," Gruening said. "My reply was that they would be paid nothing. They would have the privilege of defending their homes and their families if the enemy should come. No Eskimos ever raised that question."

After a few trips together, Gruening left the organization of the guard to Marston, who was responsible for the western half of the territory, and Scheibner, who took over the eastern half.

The two men traveled with interpreters thousands of miles by boat, airplane and dog teams along the coast and into the Interior to recruit and organize the homeland defense, including a stop in the main village on King Island in Norton Sound.

"Men and women of King Island, I am here representing the president of the United States and the governor of Alaska. You know

Villagers on King Island, many of whom volunteered for the territorial guard, built their wooden settlements on stilts on the side of cliffs among rock outcrops.

A FEW GOOD MEN

that we are at war with the Japanese," Marston said.

"I have been to Kuskokwim, Point Barrow and up to Kobuk and the Noatak rivers to visit all of you. I have seen more Eskimos than any Eskimo, and everywhere I find them to be fine people and fine Americans. They are helping in this war 100 percent.

"We need you to be the eyes and ears of the Army," he said. "You know how to hunt the seal and the walrus. You're fine shots. I want every man who is willing to join the Alaska Territorial Guard."

Marston's speeches to the people usually ended with the same statement.

"We will give you guns and ammunition. If the Japanese comes here, and lands his boat, will you shoot him quick? You men who will help your country against the Japanese, come forward now and sign your names here on this paper."

More than 6,300 Natives from 107 communities were asked to join the territorial guard, and although there was no money to pay the force and little equipment available, 100 percent enlisted, according to Alaska Territorial Guard records.

Ranging in age from 12 to 80, including 27 women, these were the original Eskimo Scouts, comprising 111 units.

A military officer swears in four Alaska Territorial Guardsmen in Barrow.

Most members of the Alaska Territorial Guard were expert shooters.

The Scouts, who were accomplished shooters, were eager to serve. Their units regularly held drills and practiced marches and shoulder arms exercises. Younger members used fake rifles in the drills, but fired real weapons at Army ranges. They were familiar with firearms through family subsistence hunts.

Gruening recalled seeing a young boy walking across the tundra near Koyuk on one of his trips. The lad had a rifle slung over his shoulder, from which four ptarmigan dangled.

"He had brought them down with that rifle – not with a shotgun," Gruening said. "He proved to be only 12 years old. He was enrolled."

And even though the government only could issue the territorial guardsmen outdated Enfield rifles, the men of the Tundra Army made every shot count.

Marston later recounted in his book a ceremony that lasted hours because all 300 men from one unit in attendance received medals as "expert marksman."

Alaska Territorial Guardsmen learned to shoot machine guns and kept watch for Japanese intruders along the coastlines.

The Inupiat and the Yup'ik soon learned the art of military reconnaissance along the shores of the Bering Sea. Young men and women routinely patrolled the coastline, keeping a sharp eye out for intruders in a war that would eventually reach Alaska by way of the Aleutians.

Alaska disbanded the Territorial Guard in 1947, with no fanfare for the volunteers who proudly wore World War I-era uniforms bearing a blue patch embroidered with gold stars of the Big Dipper and the letters ATG.

$\mathfrak{State}$ of $\mathfrak{Alaska}$

CERTIFICATE OF SERVICE

$\mathfrak{To}$ all $\mathfrak{whom}$ it $\mathfrak{may}$ concern

$\mathfrak{This}$ is to $\mathfrak{Certify}$ that

SERVED HONORABLY AND FAITHFULLY IN THE

Alaska Territorial Guard
1942-1947

GOVERNOR

SECRETARY OF STATE

This Alaska Territorial Guard Certificate was presented in 2004 to all former members of the Guard who could be located.

Guardsmen from Metlakatla to Point Barrow served with distinction and without pay until 1947 when they were disbanded "without ceremony or recognition by a war-weary nation."

Alaska's first-elected governor, William A. Egan, left, presented the Eisenhower Trophy for the state's most outstanding National Guard unit in the 1960s to Sgt. George Whitman, of Mekoryuk, representing Company B, 2nd Scout Battalion.

Also receiving awards were 1st Sgt. Theodore Booth, Kotzebue, for the outstanding training record set by Company C, 1st Scout Battalion; Sgt. Albert V. Lee, Nome, the Brig. Gen. John R. Noyes Medal as outstanding member of the 1st Scout Battalion; and Pfc. George Neck, Kasigluk, the Noyes Medal as outstanding member of the 2nd Scout Battalion. Presentations were made at Fort Richardson.

It wasn't until 2004 that the Alaska unit was officially recognized as military veterans. The U.S. Army finally granted formal military discharge certificates to former members of the Guard, which now only number about 400. And those who qualify also can receive a headstone, a U.S. flag and burial in a national military cemetery.

Many of those who came to Alaska during World War II liked what they saw and decided to set down roots in the Last Frontier. Among them was a true visionary, U.S. Army Maj. Marvin "Muktuk" Marston, who created one of Anchorage's premier recreational facilities, organized the Alaska Territorial Guard and built one of the first subdivisions in the town once known as Ship Creek.

A FEW GOOD MEN

Marvin "Muktuk" Marston – a human dynamo

Born in Tyler, Wash., in 1890, Marvin "Muktuk" Marston found himself mining copper and gold from the bush country of Northern Ontario and Quebec in the late 1930s. But when the Japanese attacked Pearl Harbor on Dec. 7, 1941, he raced to Washington, D.C., to offer officials a radical idea.

Marston, who'd spent time in Nome, proposed a plan to safeguard the nation's remaining aircraft in underground storage facilities. His creative proposal wasn't accepted, but officials saw the value of his knowledge of northern terrain and weather conditions.

In March 1941, military officials offered him a major's commission and sent him to Anchorage as a morale officer for the new base at Fort Richardson and Elmendorf Airfield. The long, dark days of Alaska winters led to one of his first missions – a snowy recreation area.

Marston rounded up a crew of avid outdoorsmen, searched the area surrounding the Anchorage Bowl and settled on an open slope valley high in the Chugach Mountains behind town for a ski development. He and the U.S. Army erected the first rope tows at what's now known as Alpenglow Arctic Valley ski area.

He continued his morale-boosting plans with a tour to military posts with comedian Joe. E. Brown. While on this trip, Marston noticed that Western Alaska lacked defenses against an enemy invasion. He believed Alaska Natives could be organized to watch for enemy activity along the territory's seaboard.

But his idea to build a Native guerrilla army to guard the coast didn't muster much support until the Japanese bombed Pearl Harbor in December 1941. Then Gov. Ernest Gruening, who'd already established citizen militias, recognized Marston as a kindred spirit and enlisted his help to organize the Alaska Territorial Guard.

While traveling to villages recruiting for the new guard, Marston earned his Eskimo name "Muktuk" after he beat a village chief in a raw whale blubber-eating contest.

Marston also earned the respect of Alaska's first people. In just a few months, he organized 111 units and personally supplied many of them with rifles and ammunition by driving to their remote locations by dog team.

After the war ended, Marston remained in Alaska and spent the rest of his life helping to build a better civilian life in Anchorage. In 1952, he and Ken Kadow built one of the community's first subdivisions, Turnagain by Sea, with a water system and paved streets to serve 150 homes. He also served as a delegate to the Constitutional Convention in 1955 and strongly advocated for Native rights.

Upon his death in 1980, at 90, Gov. William A. Egan called him "a human dynamo who dared to disturb the status quo."

8

THE FLYING BARITONE FROM FAIRBANKS

G old miners in 1906 Fairbanks passed a fur cap for contributions to give the 7-year-old warbler. His only number was "In The Good Old Summer Time," but it pleased the whiskered sourdoughs in the frontier town.

That was the beginning of a career that took the little singer far. Robert MacArthur Crawford grew up to become a professor of music, conductor of the Newark Symphony Orchestra, guest soloist for the National Symphony Orchestra in Washington, D.C., and his most enduring claim to fame, composer of the words and music of the U.S. Army Air Corps song, "Off We Go Into The Wild Blue Yonder."

Born in Dawson, Yukon Territory, during 1899, he and his family moved to the new gold camp of Fairbanks where Bob's musical talents blossomed with the opening of miners' pokes. He decided early on that he wanted to be a musician – a violinist, at first.

Bob ordered an instrument from a mail-order house, but under the teaching of Fairbanks' musician Vic Durand, he turned his atten-

Robert MacArthur Crawford sang for miners in early Fairbanks, pictured here in October 1915.

Robert Crawford spent his youth in Fairbanks singing for early settlers in the northern gold-rush town. This 1915 photo shows a street corner where the Fairbanks Clothing Store and American Bank of Alaska were built.

tion to the piano and composing. His musical composition ability soon became evident when he wrote the words and music for a song titled "My Northland."

An energetic youngster, Bob sold newspapers to earn money during the early 1900s as he knew he wanted to continue his education Outside. A construction job on the Alaska Railroad, and another job at a service station, earned him enough for one year at Princeton University. While studying at Princeton, he also took part in many extracurricular activities and started the Princeton University Orchestra. For seven years, he directed and orchestrated the music of the annual Triangle Show, and demand for his baritone voice grew.

Following graduation, he won a scholarship to the school of Conservatoire American at Fontainebleau in France. The school started with the involvement of the United States in World War I when

Robert MacArthur Crawford flew to Fairbanks in 1936 and performed at the Empress Theatre, the building seen here with the mural painted on the side near the Mecca. It was located on Second Street between Cushman and Lacy streets.

Brig. Gen. John Pershing wanted to improve the quality of U.S. military band music. Walter Damrosch, then conductor of the New York Philharmonic, was asked to organize a school in Chaumont, France, where American troops were based.

Bob also earned a scholarship to Juilliard Graduate School in New York.

The young musician developed another passion during this time – aviation. He piloted his bride around Alaska on their honeymoon, and then flew back to Fairbanks in 1936, bringing light opera soprano Ruby Mercer with him. They presented a concert in the old Empress Theatre, with Don Adler as piano accompanist.

Crawford's love for flying and the wild, blue yonder prompted him to enter a contest to find a song for the U.S. Army Air Corps.

The contest was the brainchild of Assistant Chief of the Air Corps Brig. Gen. Hap Arnold and Chief of the Air Corps Maj. Gen. Oscar Westover. In 1937, it was sponsored by Liberty Magazine.

More than 750 compositions flooded the volunteer committee,

chaired by Mildred Yount, wife of a senior Air Corps officer. But committee members found no songs that satisfied them.

So Arnold, who took over command of the Air Corps in 1938, solicited direct inquiries from contestants – including Irving Berlin. But no new creations proved worthy, either.

Fairbanks' own Robert MacArthur Crawford won the 1939 contest for a U.S. Army Air Corps theme song.

Then, just before the July 1939 deadline, Crawford entered his song. It fit the bill, and the committee unanimously voted it as the winner.

But not everyone liked the number.

At a dinner party during September 1939, the committee shared a recording of the song with famous aviator Charles Lindberg. And although he showed favor for the song at the time, a diary entry showed he really didn't care much for it.

"I think it is mediocre at best," Lindberg wrote. "Neither the music nor the words appealed to me."

Crawford, known by now as the "Flying Baritone," was handed the $1,000 first-place prize at the 1939 National Air races in Cleveland, Ohio. He then stepped to the microphone and sang the song for the first time in public.

Hundreds of top military and civilian celebrities attending the aviation banquet stood and applauded the song that epitomized the cocky determination and enthusiasm of the men who became World War II fliers – including Crawford, who joined the Air Corps at the outbreak of the war and rose to the rank of lieutenant colonel.

It wasn't until 1965 that an Air Force Scroll of Appreciation was awarded to Crawford – the first official recognition by the Air Force of the writer of the famed flying song.

It was awarded posthumously, for Crawford had died on March 12, 1961, in New York City. His widow, Hester, accepted it on behalf of the Flying Baritone, the "Sourdough Kid" who had never been so happy as when he was making music and climbing into the wild, blue yonder.

On July 30, 1971, Apollo 15 launched from NASA Kennedy Space Center in Florida at 9:34 a.m. A few days later, the *Falcon* lunar module carried Col. David R. Scott, Lt. Col. James B. Irwin and the first page of the score written by Robert MacArthur Crawford to the surface of the moon.

As the *Falcon* blasted off the moon following its successful mission, Maj. Alfred M. Worden – who had a tape recorder on board the orbiting *Endeavor* command module – broadcast a rendition of the song to the world.

Scott, Irwin and Worden comprised the first and only all-U.S. Air Force Apollo crew and arranged to take the sheet music with them as a tribute to Crawford and the Air Force.

Official U.S. Air Force Song

Off we go into the wild blue yonder,
Climbing high into the sun;
Here they come zooming to meet our thunder,
At 'em boys, Give 'er the gun!
Down we dive, spouting our flame from under,
Off with one hell of a roar!
We live in fame or go down in flame.
Nothing'll stop the U.S. Air Force!

Minds of men fashioned a crate of thunder,
Sent it high into the blue;
Hands of men blasted the world asunder;
How they lived God only knew! (God only knew!)
Souls of men dreaming of skies to conquer
Gave us wings, ever to soar!
With scouts before and bombers galore.
Nothing'll stop the U.S. Air Force!

Here's a hot toast to the host
Of those who love the vastness of the sky,
To a friend we send a message of his brother men who fly.
We drink to those who gave their all of old,
Then down we roar to score the rainbow's pot of gold.
A toast to the host of men we boast, the U.S. Air Force!

Off we go into the wild sky yonder,
Keep the wings level and true;
If you'd live to be a grey-haired wonder
Keep the nose out of the blue! (Out of the blue, boy!)
Flying men, guarding the nation's border,
We'll be there, followed by more!
In echelon we carry on.
Nothing can stop the U.S. Air Force!

9

J. Doolittle: Nome Town Boy

"Nome Town Boy Makes Good" proclaimed the Nome Nugget headline in April 1942. One of Nome's own, U.S. Army Air Forces pilot Lt. Col. James Doolittle, had led the Tokyo bombing raid in World War II.

Doolittle was known among the people of Nome as the cute little boy who started selling Nome Nugget newspapers at the age of 7. And perhaps the fighting spirit and pluck that earned him so much fame in later years got its start in Nome, too. This boy, small for his age and with long, curly hair, met challenges from teasing schoolchildren head on.

This is the scene that may have met the eyes of Jimmy Doolittle and his mother when they stepped ashore at Nome during the summer of 1900.

A FEW GOOD MEN

Jimmy Doolittle's father, Frank, searched in vain for riches in the Klondike before heading to Nome in 1900.

Life in Nome was harsh and challenging in 1900. Jimmy's father, Frank, had arrived in the new golden city that year, after vainly looking for gold in the Klondike. Although he had left his wife and infant son, James Harold – born on Dec. 14, 1896 – behind in California when he set out in search of riches, he sent for them after he reached the new Alaska gold camp.

Three-year-old Jimmy and his mother came ashore at Nome in the summer of 1900. A solid phalanx of tents stretched along the black sands that had washed up from the Bering Sea. But there was still not enough housing for the thousands of gold seekers.

Turn-of-the-last-century Nome was one of the most lawless mining camps in the world. It was the paradise of thieves, thugs, cheats, outlaws and the most degraded type of sporting women and their parasites, according to reports at the time. And U.S. infantry troops that were brought in couldn't make much headway against the lawlessness and corruption.

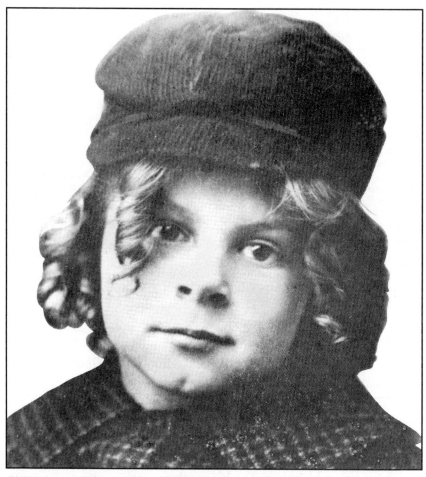
Children teased little Jimmy Doolittle, seen here, because he had long, curly hair.

"On the board sidewalks at night you had to step around the sprawled-out figures of men – sometimes asleep – sometimes dead drunk – once in a while they were dead," according to Phyllis Downing Carlson, who researched Nome's gold-rush days.

Builders were much in demand, however, and Frank Doolittle, a competent carpenter, found plenty of work. He kept busy building houses for those with money to pay him, and in his spare time, he managed to build one for his family – an unpainted wooden building that had to be straightened up each spring when the ground thawed.

A FEW GOOD MEN

While those who lived in Nome faced a bitter battle for survival in the harsh arctic environment, Jimmy also found himself in a battle for survival against other boys who made fun of his long, girl-like curls.

After his first day of school, Jimmy demanded that his curls be cut off. His mother complied, but scrappy Jimmy still found that his reputation demanded he keep on fighting. Any small boy could be taken into the gang if he could lick little Jimmy Doolittle.

Wiry, tough Jimmy more than held his own. With many fights to his credit, he learned early in life to take care of himself.

When he learned that dog-team drivers and runners were looked up to in gold-rush Nome, he decided to be a runner, since he didn't have any dogs. And he'd run until he collapsed. Years later, doctors diagnosed a heart murmur deemed caused by over-exertion when he was young. But even in those days, the word "quit" wasn't in Jimmy's vocabulary.

When Jimmy Doolittle started attending Nome school, seen here in 1906, he told his mother to cut his hair because the children teased him.

When Jimmy turned 7, he and his father made a trip to Seattle. It was his first taste of city life, and he loved it. Automobiles, trains, trolley cars – even painted houses. He decided he would like to be a part of that exciting life.

As soon as the pair returned to Nome, Jimmy found a job selling the Nome Nugget to earn money. He started reading everything he could lay his hands on, too.

It was 1908 before his dream of seeing the outside world again came true. He and his mother left for California, leaving his father to the great Alaska adventure. Frank Doolittle died in 1917, still seeking the gold that always eluded him.

While Jimmy and his mother made Los Angeles their home, the small boy continued his scrappy ways and became known for his ability as a fighter. He learned how to box and became amateur bantamweight champion of the West Coast in 1912 at age 15.

Around the same time he saw his first airplane and became interested in aviation. When World War I came along in 1917, Jimmy enlisted in the Signal Corps Reserve, Aviation Section, hoping to go

Jimmy Doolittle and his mother moved to California in 1908. He's seen here sitting behind the wheel of a REO, with grandparents Mr. and Mrs. Wilber Bell relegated to the back seat.

A FEW GOOD MEN

overseas. In January 1918, he was ordered to begin flight training at Rockwell Field in San Diego.

That was the beginning of a career that took him to the heights. Although his desire to get into combat during the war wasn't realized, he did set a record for crossing the continent in 1922, acquired one of the first doctoral degrees in aeronautical engineering and won the coveted Schneider trophy, the Harmon trophy and the Bendix trophy.

James Doolittle, seen here after World War I, became interested in aviation early in life.

The Air Line Pilots Association accorded him honorary membership in its association in 1971 and its president, John J. O'Donnell, said:

"You led the way in aviation when it was an unknown quantity to us. You made our job easier and safer. ..."

The pinnacle of his distinguished career in World War II was becoming Commander-in-Chief of the Air Forces in North Africa and the Eighth Air Force during the Normandy Invasion – and of course, leader of the famous raiders that took off from the aircraft carrier *Hornet* and successfully bombed Tokyo on April 18, 1942.

He helped boost morale across America and headlines around the country proclaimed, "Tokyo Bombed. Doolittle Doo'd It!"

And the little Nome Nugget headlines proclaimed the fact, too. The hometown boy had made good.

Doolittle, who served as a brigadier general, major general and lieutenant general during his career with the U.S. Army Air Forces, earned the Medal of Honor for his valor and leadership as commander of the Doolittle Raid while he was a lieutenant colonel.

"For conspicuous leadership above and beyond the call of duty, involving personal valor and intrepidity at an extreme hazard to life," his citation read. "With the apparent certainty of being forced to land in enemy territory or to perish at sea, Lt. Col. Doolittle personally led a squadron of Army bombers, manned by volunteer crews, in a highly destructive raid on the Japanese mainland."

While the Doolittle Raid is viewed by historians as a major morale-building victory for the United States, it did little damage to the Japanese war industry. But the raid showed the Japanese that their homeland was vulnerable to air attack and forced them to withdraw several frontline fighter units from Pacific war zones for homeland defense.

U.S. Army Air Forces Lt. Col. James Doolittle, seen here leaning out of a cockpit window, led the 1942 bombing attack on Tokyo.

More significantly, Japanese commanders considered the raid deeply embarrassing. Their attempt to close the perceived gap in their Pacific defense perimeter led directly to the decisive American victory during the Battle of Midway in June 1942. It also led to the invasion of Alaska's Aleutian Islands – where the Japanese believed Doolittle had originated his attack.

When President Franklin D. Roosevelt was asked from where the attack was launched, he humorously said its base was Shangri-la, a fictional paradise from the popular novel "Lost Horizon." Later, the U.S. Navy named one of its carriers the *USS Shangri-la*.

Jimmy Doolittle died on Sept. 27, 1993, at 96.

A FEW GOOD MEN

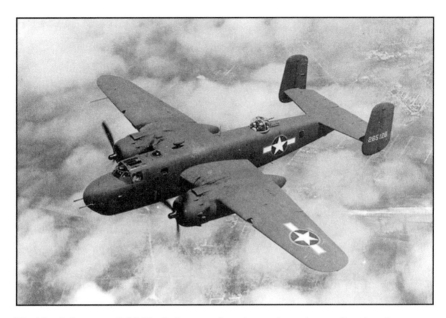

The North American B-25 Mitchell was an American twin-engine medium bomber manufactured by North American Aviation. It was used with devastating effect against German and Japanese targets in every combat theater of World War II. The aircraft was named the "Mitchell" in honor of Gen. William "Billy" Mitchell, an early air-power pioneer and advocate of an independent U.S. Air Force. It is the only American military aircraft named after a specific person. By the end of its production, more than 10,000 B-25s in several models had been built. These included a few limited variations, such as the U.S. Navy's PBJ-1 patrol bomber and the Army Air Forces F-10 photo reconnaissance aircraft.

The B-25 was flown by the Army Air Forces and the Navy, as well as many Allied forces that included Australia, the United Kingdom – which received more than 900 – China, the Netherlands and the Soviet Union.

The B-25 first gained fame as the bomber used in the April 1942 Doolittle Raid, in which 16 B-25Bs, led by the legendary Lt. Col. Jimmy Doolittle, took off from the carrier USS Hornet and successfully bombed Tokyo and four other Japanese cities without loss to themselves. However, 15 of the planes subsequently crash-landed in Eastern China en route to their recovery fields in that country. These losses were the result of fuel exhaustion, stormy nighttime conditions with zero visibility, and the lack of electronic homing aids at the recovery bases. Only one B-25B landed intact; it came down in Russia, where its five-man crew was interned and the aircraft confiscated. Three crewmen died while ditching their planes, and four of 10 crewmen captured by the Japanese and held in prisoner of war camps were executed. Sixty-eight of the 80 Doolittle Raid crewmen survived their historic mission and eventually made it back to American lines.

Source: U.S. Air Force

CONFLICT IN THE ALEUTIANS

10

DUTCH HARBOR ATTACKED

Dutch Harbor families awoke early on June 3, 1942, unaware that their world was about to explode. But soon the drone of Japanese Zeros mixed with the sounds of coffee pots and teakettles on the boil to crack the silence of the dawn. By 5:45 a.m., more than a dozen bombers and fighters were screaming over their town.

"Out of the blue, real bombs began to fall," recalled one longtime resident.

This article announcing the June 3, 1942, attack on Dutch Harbor was the only news to break about the Japanese raid in the Aleutian Chain.

The U.S. military placed a blackout on any more news as it feared the American public would panic and think the Japanese were ready to invade their homes.

Japanese troops invaded the Aleutian Islands, only 750 miles north of their homeland, in June 1942.

U.S. forces at Fort Mears met the attack with anti-aircraft and small arms fire. They downed two Japanese planes.

Another attack at 9 a.m. targeted five U.S. destroyers sighted by a Japanese fighter plane on the first attack. But dense fog closed in and concealed their objective.

On June 4, nine Japanese fighters and 17 bombers again struck Dutch Harbor, located on Unalaska Island. They scored direct hits on the fuel docks, the hospital and the small naval facility at Fort Mears.

Eight American P-40s, launched from a secret base on Umnak Island, engaged the Japanese planes in aerial dogfights. The surprise counter-attack downed four enemy dive-bombers and one Zero.

During the two-day attack, 33 U.S. soldiers and sailors, as well as 10 civilians, died.

But the devastation at Dutch Harbor could have been worse.

Above: Fog often rolled into Dutch Harbor, seen above, and caused problems for both the Americans and the Japanese during World War II.

Below: Japanese bombs fell on Fort Mears at Dutch Harbor on June 3-4, 1942.

Above: Enemy bombs destroyed the hospital at Dutch Harbor on June 4, 1942. Patients had been moved to bomb shelters, so there was no loss of life.

Right: The beached barracks ship SS *Northwestern* burned after being attacked by the Japanese.

Five American bi-wings and two PBYs, nicknamed "Catalina" airplanes, sit on the runway at Fort Mears in Dutch Harbor.

Rear Adm. Kakuji Kakuta had dispatched more than 30 planes from two small aircraft carriers, the *Ryujo* and *Junyo*, hidden in the waters off Unalaska. Due to fog, high seas and strong winds, less than half the planes reached the island.

Capture of the Aleutians first appeared as a Japanese goal in a plan prepared by Adm. Isoroku Yamamoto, according to the U.S. Army Center of Military History. Yamamoto intended to "invade and occupy strategic points in the Western Aleutians," as well as Midway Island on the western tip of the Hawaiian island chain.

Yamamoto saw these two sites as anchors for a defensive perimeter in the north and central Pacific. By using the Aleutians and Midway as bait, the Japanese commander also intended to lure the already weakened American fleet from Pearl Harbor and destroy it before new construction could replace the losses sustained on Dec. 7, 1941.

And after 16 U.S. bombers led by Lt. Col. James H. Doolittle

CONFLICT IN THE ALEUTIANS

took off from the carrier *Hornet* and bombed Tokyo on April 18, Japanese leaders made capturing islands in the Aleutian Chain a priority. The Imperial High Command thought the American raid had started out from a secret base in the western Aleutians.

Japanese planners also thought the United States had extensive military installations at Dutch Harbor and smaller garrisons on Adak, Kiska and Attu.

The Americans actually had little military support in the Aleutians at the time of the attack. A secret field at Fort Glenn, disguised as a cannery on Umnak Island, housed about 2,300 combat troops, Fort Randall at Cold Bay around 2,500, including

U.S. Army Air Forces Lt. Col. James H. Doolittle wired a Japanese medal to a bomb destined for Tokyo in retaliation for the attack on Pearl Harbor.

Doolittle, dubbed the "Babe Ruth of the Flyboys," spent part of his youth in Nome during its gold rush beginning in 1899.

engineer troops, and Fort Mears a little more than 6,000.

But supplying those air fields with modern aircraft was not easy. While many pursuit and medium bombardment planes headed north along the Northwest Staging Route through Canada during the first months of 1942, many crashed en route – mostly due to inexperienced pilots. By early March, only half the pursuits and a quarter of the bombers arrived in tact and were ready for combat duty, according to the U.S. Army Center of Military History.

American code breakers learned in mid-March that the Japanese planned to bomb, and then occupy, the Aleutians. The decoded mes-

This aerial view of Cold Bay on May 16, 1942, shows the U.S. military gearing up for a possible attack by the Japanese.

sages also revealed that the main thrust of the Japanese attack would be Midway, so that's where the Americans sent the majority of its fleet.

Intercepts in May pinpointed Dutch Harbor as the main target in the Aleutians. The messages also gave U.S. military officials the strength of the Japanese Northern Area Force and put the planned attack date around June 1.

The U.S. military responded quickly and moved planes forward to the new Alaska Peninsula air bases, where supplies of gasoline and bombs had been stockpiled. By June 1, one heavy and six medium bombers and 17 fighter planes were sitting on Umnak and six bombers and 16 fighters at Cold Bay.

The Navy also reacted to the threat of a Japanese attack, placing five cruisers, 14 destroyers and six submarines off Kodiak. It put eight radar-equipped patrol planes at Dutch Harbor, as well.

One of those patrol planes spotted the enemy through thick fog about 400 miles south of Kiska on June 2. Early the next morning, the Japanese launched their attack on Dutch Harbor.

In the second Japanese attack on Dutch Harbor on June 4, 1942, one Zero did not return to the carrier *Ryujo*. Hit by a U.S. Navy PBY, it made a forced landing on Akutan and was recovered and shipped to North Island Naval Air Station in San Diego for examination.

The information gleaned from this efficient machine highlighted shortcomings in U.S. aircraft design, and many of the features in the Mitsubishi A6M Zero then were incorporated into the successful Navy F6-F Grumman Hellcat.

Secrets learned from studying the aircraft's strengths and weaknesses helped Allied pilots battle it in wartime skies.

Following that two-day assault, the enemy's fleet disappeared into the Aleutian weather and found refuge in Japanese waters.

U.S. amphibious and bomber aircraft searched the Pacific Ocean for any sign of the attackers. But bad weather and low visibility exacted a heavy toll on the searchers. Of six Catalinas that came within sight of the Japanese fleet, four were downed by enemy fire and another lost to the fog.

Another Japanese fleet, commanded by Boshiro Hosogaya, appeared on June 6 and occupied the island of Kiska. The following day, the enemy invaded Attu.

11

ENEMY INVADES ATTU

The remote islands of the Aleutian Chain, home to the Unangan people for more than 8,000 years, endured the first invasion on American soil since the War of 1812.

On June 6, 1942, two days after the attack on Dutch Harbor, a Japanese special landing party and 500 troops came ashore at Kiska

Japanese troops raise the Imperial battle flag on Kiska after landing on June 6, 1942.

CONFLICT IN THE ALEUTIANS

Aleutian Chain Offers Challenging Terrain and Weather

There are approximately 120 volcanic islands comprising the Aleutian Chain, which stretches from the tip of the Alaska Peninsula to within 90 miles of Kamchatka, Russia. The islands are rocky, barren and covered with spongy tundra or swampy muskeg.

The easternmost island, Unimak, is also the largest, measuring 65 by 22 miles. To the southwest is Unalaska, on which Dutch Harbor is located. Unalaska is about 2,000 miles from both San Francisco and Honolulu.

Continuing westward, in order, lie Umnak, Atka and Adak. Kiska lies 610 miles west of Dutch Harbor. Farther west is Shemya, a two- by four-mile island located about 35 miles east of Attu. Its highest point is about 240 feet.

Attu, pictured above, is the westernmost American island. Located nearly 1,100 miles from Alaska's mainland and 750 miles northeast of the northernmost of the Japanese Kurile islands, it has a land mass of about 20 by 35 miles. The island has high mountainous terrain, rising 3,000 feet, starting close to its shoreline and stretching into the interior of the island.

Attu usually has a cold, damp fog accompanied by snow or icy rain. Average rainfall measures between 40-50 inches a year. And squalls, called "williwaws," often sweep down the mountains. Winds can reach velocities of more than 100 miles an hour in minutes.

Both the Japanese and American military forces were plagued by the treacherous Aleutian terrain and weather during World War II.

Japanese soldiers gather around their tank after invading Kiska in June 1942.

around 10:30 p.m. They captured a small American naval weather detachment of 10 men, along with a dog. One member of the detachment escaped, but surrendered after 50 days – thin, starving and cold.

The enemy then invaded Attu at 3 a.m. on June 7.

Villagers, who'd been expecting American evacuation ships, instead found themselves running from bullets that Sunday morning. Thousands of Japanese troops poured over the hills surrounding the village of Chichagof – shooting as they came and wounding several villagers.

"The Japs are here," screamed an Aleut woman amid a hail of bullets as she rushed into the cabin of Bureau of Indian Affairs teacher Etta Jones.

Jones' husband, a 60-year-old radio technician who operated a government radio and weather-reporting station, began transmitting messages of the attack to Dutch Harbor.

Soon the Japanese were on the couple's doorstep, and the Jones' surrendered. Most sources agree that Charles Foster Jones was taken by the enemy and never seen again.

The villagers were all rounded up and herded to the schoolhouse. Once they all were accounted for, the Japanese allowed them to return to their homes, said Olean Prokopeuff (Golodoff) in a story that appeared in an Aleutian/Pribilof Islands Association Inc. article for Aang Angagin. Prokopeuff, who lived through the event, said bayonet-carrying enemy soldiers guarded them.

The Japanese kept the Aleut fishermen busy for three days supplying the troops with food. Then the villagers were told to grab some food and personal items for themselves, because they were leaving the island. Prokopeuff said she then watched as Japanese soldiers burned her home.

Etta Jones, 62, and the village's 40-plus Aleuts were transported in the hold of a freighter to Hokkaido, Japan, for internment. Prokopeuff said they were kept in the unpleasant-smelling hold for the week-long voyage, never seeing daylight until they reached Japan.

Jones was separated from the Natives and interred at Yokohama, along with U.S. Navy personnel captured on Kiska, while the Aleuts were interred at Otaru, Hokkaido.

Charles Foster Jones and wife Etta, seen here holding two puppies, were the only white couple living on Attu when the Japanese invaded in June 1942. He was killed and Etta was taken prisoner and shipped to Japan.

Black smoke rises and then hangs over Kiska Harbor after U.S. bombs strike a Japanese transport during a raid.

Several Attuan detainees later recalled their living conditions in Japan.

"[We] were housed in a large building, supervised by a Japanese policeman, who lived in partitioned rooms in the same building," they said in "Personal Justice Denied," a 1982 government report issued by the Commission on Wartime Relocation and Internment of Civilians.

"The Aleuts had no freedom, [and were] held in the same building for the entire war, except the ones who worked in a clay pit near by. The buildings were heated by coal stoves in winter. Hot baths were available whenever the Aleuts wanted them. They slept on the floor on the Japanese standard mats 'Tatami' and they had plenty of blankets."

Tuberculosis later spread widely among the Attuans, despite monthly visits to their camp by a doctor who gave routine examinations and inoculations. Many died.

"The loss of their high-protein diet and fresh food, aggravated by short rations, caused malnutrition and starvation during the last year of their captivity," the commission report said. "As the war dragged on, Japan was starved for resources; Japanese troops and the Attuans' guards alike faced shortages."

Half of the Alaska Native prisoners died in Japan. When World War II ended, the surviving 21 Aleuts and one newborn returned to Alaska. Some settled in Akutan, none returned to Attu.

After the Japanese military invaded Attu and sent the Aleuts on their way to Japan, it settled in to defend its position on the island.

While it's widely believed that Japanese leaders had initially intended to set up a defensive perimeter stretching from the Aleutians to Midway Island, some question why – after their devastating defeat at Midway – they decided to entrench themselves at Attu and Kiska.

American bombs soon started falling on the islands of Kiska and Attu, seen above, in an attempt to rout the Japanese military from the Aleutian Islands.

Most military and historical sources agree that the Japanese still regarded their occupation in the Aleutians as a valuable deterrent to an attack on Japan from the north.

The Japanese garrisons on Kiska and Attu, which numbered more than 11,000 troops, set up defensive positions and began watching for attacks from the Americans, who began bombing raids with U.S. Navy PBYs on Kiska from Atka on June 11. The U.S. Army Air Forces followed with attacks on Kiska beginning June 12.

As Japanese soldiers dug in to repel attacks from the U.S. military, Japanese Americans were being evicted from the territory.

12

JAPANESE-AMERICANS INTERRED

Following the Japanese attacks on Pearl Harbor, and later Dutch Harbor, Kiska and Attu, wartime hysteria and fear of sabotage and espionage ran rampant across the country. President Franklin D. Roosevelt signed Executive Order 9066 in February 1942. It ordered the removal of more than 112,000 Japanese-Americans from the West Coast. Those with Japanese ancestry were taken from their homes, businesses and schools and put in internment camps.

After a short stay at Fort Richardson near Anchorage, Alaska's

Japanese-Americans from Alaska were sent to the Minidoka Relocation Center, seen here, located in Idaho.

193 detainees were transferred to the Puyallup Assembly Center in Washington state. They then boarded trains bound for the Minidoka Relocation Center in Idaho.

The Minidoka internment camp, 20 miles northeast of Twin Falls, was built on a dry, desolate plain. It housed those of Japanese ancestry from Alaska, Washington and Oregon, as well as 50 seal and whale hunters who were half Alaska Native, according to the National Park Service.

When the detainees arrived at the camp in August 1942, they found it still under construction with no running water or sewer system.

"When we first arrived here we almost cried, and thought that this is the land God had forgotten," one evacuee wrote to friends. "The vast expanse of nothing but sagebrush and dust, a landscape so alien to our eyes, and a desolate, woebegone feeling of being so far removed from home and fireside bogged us down mentally, as well as physically."

The camp's superintendent of education also saw the despair in the detainees.

This aerial military photograph shows the Japanese relocation camp of Minidoka in the dusty plains of Idaho.

Children of detainees in Minidoka play outdoors in a barren environment surrounded by tar paper-covered barracks.

"... these people are living in the midst of a desert where they see nothing except tar paper-covered barracks, sagebrush, and rocks. No flowers, no trees, no shrubs, no grass," wrote Arthur Klienkopf in a diary. "The impact of emotional disturbance as a result of the evacuation . . . plus this dull, dreary existence in a desert region surely must give these people a feeling of helplessness, hopelessness, and despair which we on the outside do not and will never fully understand."

There were shortages of food and medicine in the camps, which meant many sick people were left untreated. Some died. At least five other internees were shot and killed because of illness or because they tried to escape, according to government records.

About 60 percent of those interred at Minidoka were U.S. born American citizens. The remainder, born in Japan, had not yet become naturalized citizens.

For almost two years, the country detained them because the government questioned their loyalty. But even though these Japanese-

Minidoka, one of 10 internment camps for Japanese-Americans in the United States, re-sembled a prison with poor food, cramped quarters and communal facilities. The government provided barracks without plumbing or cooking facilities.

The camp, which covered 35,000 acres, was plagued by dust storms that could be painful for the inhabitants of the camp. But Minidoka was regarded as the "best" of the camps. The positive atmosphere of the camp came from its relatively homogeneous population and friendly administration. It opened on Aug. 10, 1942, and closed on Oct. 28, 1945.

Americans endured hardships while being interred, their loyalty to the United States remained steadfast. About 1,000 volunteered to serve in the military – dozens died for their country.

And when it was all said and done, only 10 Americans were convicted of spying for Japan during the war – all Caucasian.

Harold L. Ickes, Roosevelt's Secretary of the Interior, later lamented the role the administration played in the fate of America's Japanese people.

"As a member of President Roosevelt's administration, I saw

the United States Army give way to mass hysteria over the Japanese ... it lost its self-control, and egged on by public clamor, some of it from greedy Americans ... it began to round up indiscriminately the Japanese who had been born in Japan, as well as those born here," he said.

"Crowded into cars like cattle, these helpless people were hurried away to hastily constructed and thoroughly inadequate concentration camps, with soldiers with nervous muskets on guard, in the Great American desert. We gave the fancy names of 'relocation centers' to these dust bowls, but they were concentration camps nonetheless. ..."

Most Alaskans could not believe their Japanese neighbors were enemy spies. So in the spirit of friendship and caring, they watched over the homes and businesses of those removed from the territory. But only about 80 of the almost 200 Alaska detainees returned north after the war ended.

Another group of Alaskans suffered, also.

U.S. authorities evacuated hundreds of men, women and children from the Aleutian and Pribilof islands following the Japanese attacks on Dutch Harbor, Kiska and Attu. These people were relocated to "duration villages" in Southeast Alaska.

13

ALEUTS BECOME REFUGEES

Hunger. Disease. Death. Hardly words that people associate with places of safety. But they are the words used by many Aleut people to describe their experience while living in "duration villages" during World War II.

After the Japanese bombed Unalaska, occupied Kiska and invaded Attu in June 1942, the U.S. military ordered a hasty evacuation of more than 800 Alaska Natives living in the Aleutian and Pribilof islands.

U.S. bombs dropped on the island of Kiska left substantial craters in the earth.

CONFLICT IN THE ALEUTIANS

U.S. sailors burned the village of Atka, seen here in 1938, so the Japanese could not benefit from the shelters on the island.

At 8 a.m. on June 12, U.S. Navy seaplane tender *Gillis* received orders to evacuate Atka and burn the village. But when sailors came ashore, they only found Office of Indian Affairs schoolteacher Ruby Magee and her husband, Ralph.

The couple had urged the villagers to hide after listening to 18 hours of bombing raids on Kiska and sighting a Japanese scout plane.

"We had the people move out to their fish camps about three miles from the village, thinking that they might be safer out there in their tents," Ruby Magee said, according to "Personal Justice Denied," a 1982 report by the Commission on Wartime Relocation and Internment of Civilians.

The Navy gave the Magees 20 minutes to pack and then sent seamen to burn the village, including the church, so the Japanese could not use the buildings. When the Atka Aleuts returned to their village later that evening, they found their possessions destroyed. Only four houses were untouched.

The crew of the *USS Hulbert* spotted the villagers and loaded them on board. The ship carried the 62 Aleuts to Nikolski village, on Umnak Island. The people later were taken to Dutch Harbor.

The U.S. attack transport *Delarof*, in the distance, took evacuees from St. Paul to Dutch Harbor in June 1942.

On June 15, U.S. Army Transport *Delarof* arrived in the Pribilof Islands to evacuate St. George and St. Paul. The U.S. Fish and Wildlife Service agent and caretaker of St. George prepared the village.

"I was first instructed to prepare the village for destruction that night by placing a pail of gasoline in each house and building, and a charge of dynamite for each other installation such as storage tanks, light plants, trucks, radio transmitters, receivers, antenna masts, etc.," Daniel C.R. Benson later said. "The packing of everybody was to be very simple – absolutely nothing but one suitcase per person and a roll of blankets."

The *Delarof* pulled into Dutch Harbor, on the island of Unalaska, the next day and unloaded the Pribilof people.

But the evacuees couldn't stay there. Unalaska faced a food shortage with the influx of so many people.

On June 18, the military loaded all the evacuees on board the *Delarof* and sent them on their way to an unknown future. As the ship steamed from the dock, military officials scrambled to come up with a plan and places to put them.

Many of the people who boarded the *Delarof* for the journey away from the Aleutians did not speak English. They had no idea what was happening to them.

Men, women and children huddled together in the ship's hold, healthy and sick packed close to each other. The first casualty, a baby born en route that contracted pneumonia, was buried at sea in the Gulf of Alaska near Kodiak, according to government records.

Fish and Wildlife Service nurse Fredrika Martin later recalled the tragedy.

"Since once aboard the ship, the St. George doctor felt completely free of responsibility for his islanders and had no personal interest in any of these patients of his, he could not be coaxed into the disagreeable hold even before all the Aleuts and many non-Aleuts came down after our stay-over at Dutch Harbor with 'ship's cold,' a serious grippe infection," Martin said.

"He did not come to assist even at the birth of a St. George baby or its subsequent death of bronchial pneumonia because of our inability [Dr. Berenberg's and mine] to separate mother and child from other grippe-sufferers, and the mother herself was ill," Martin said. "I think I recall this doctor attending the midnight or after funeral of the poor little mite, such a tiny weighted parcel being let down into the deep waters of the Gulf of Alaska against a shoreline of dramatic peaks and blazing sunset sky."

Young Aleut men push boats ashore at their new home, Killisnoo, in Southeast Alaska.

St. Paul residents lived at this abandoned cannery in Funter Bay during World War II.

Since time was of the essence, authorities chose to settle the evacuees in five separate camps in Southeast Alaska, 1,500 miles away from the Aleutians. They decided to drop entire villages at different locations. Atkans were assigned an abandoned cannery on Killisnoo Island and the Pribilof people were to settle deserted facilities nearby.

All 480 Pribilof residents debarked in Funter Bay, a two-mile-long bay on the western side of Admiralty Island, on June 24. Evacuees from St. Paul were housed in an abandoned fish cannery and the community of St. George in an abandoned gold mining camp a few miles away.

Some of the buildings at the fish cannery, which had been unused for more than a dozen years, were so rotten that people fell through floors, according to testimony later given. Families lived in poorly insulated rooms, partitioned by blankets. Rats and mice often scurried across the bare floors.

One toilet, which sat over the beach just above the low tide mark, served 90 percent of the evacuees. All the human waste washed directly into the bay, contaminating the water.

Food was scarce. And until that fall, people slept in relays.

"We have as many as ten and thirteen people, large and small, sleeping, or trying to sleep, in one room ...," wrote L.C. McMillin, agent and caretaker of the Pribilof evacuation camp at Funter Bay, in a letter to Edward C. Johnston, superintendent of the U.S. Fish and Wildlife Service.

"… No brooms, soap, mops or brushes to keep the place suitable for pigs to sleep in. It seems funny that our government can drop so many people in a place like this and then forget about them altogether. … If you think that this is any fun, you should be here," McMillin wrote.

In October, the women of St. Paul also wrote a petition in protest of the conditions at the camp.

"We the people of this place wants a better place … to live. This … is no place for a living creature. We drink impure water and then get sick, the children's get skin disease, even the grown ups are sick from cold.

"We ate from the mess house and it is near the toilet only a few yards away. We eat the filth that is flying around.

"We got no place to take a bath and no place to wash our clothes or dry them when it rains. We women are always lugging water up stairs and take turns warming it up and the stove is small. We live in a room with our children just enough to turn around in. We used blankets for walls just to live in private. We need clothes and shoes for our children, how are we going to clothe them with just a few dollars. …

Evacuees from St. George spent World War II living in this abandoned gold mine at Funter Bay in Southeast Alaska.

"Why they not take us to a better place to live and work for ourselves and live in a better house. Men and women are very eager to work. When winter come it still would be worse with water all frozen up. ... Do we have to see our children suffer. We all have rights to speak for ourselves."

But conditions did not substantially improve at Funter Bay until the winter of 1943-44, 1-1/2 years after the Aleuts had been evacuated, according to the commission report.

Those housed at the abandoned Admiralty Alaska Gold Mine three miles away didn't fare much better.

One two-story un-partitioned building housed 10 families, a total of 46 people. A new mess house was used as a storeroom, canteen and church, according to the commission report. Above the mess hall, 26 single men lived in a low loft accessible only through an outside entrance. The other Pribilof people occupied another two-story dormitory similar to the one at the cannery, but the 20 families living there had no heat.

And although the camps had no cook stoves, plumbing fixtures, water tanks or other necessary equipment and supplies that would make life bearable, the assistant fishery supervisor wrote to the Alaska fisheries chief that all was well.

Life was not easy for the Aleut refugees sent to Southeast Alaska during World War II.

Schoolteachers Ruby and Ralph Magee managed the camp filled with the people of Atka at Killisnoo.

"We feel that Mr. Johnston has the situation well in hand insofar as the Pribilof natives and whites are concerned and predict that his Funter Bay camp will serve as a model for others to be established later."

The Atkans who landed at Killisnoo on June 25 faced difficulties, as well, but their accommodations were a bit better. The camp, which was managed by the Magees, had cabins and houses outfitted with stoves and cots.

The camp also had an abundant supply of driftwood for heating, a laundry, one bathtub and three toilets for the 80 evacuees. And most

The village of Akutan was evacuated and houses were boarded up.

of the able-bodied men found employment at the government's supply base at Excursion Inlet, the forestry department, nearby canneries or signed on with the military.

On June 29, the Navy ordered the evacuation of all Natives with at least one-eighth Aleut blood from the Aleutian Islands. In a sweep eastward from Atka to Akutan, the Aleut villages of Nikolski on Umnak Island; Makushin, Biorka, Chernofski and Kashega on Unalaska Island; and Akutan on Akutan Island were evacuated.

Most of these evacuees only received a few hours notice to pack necessities.

"In 1942, my wife and our four children were whipped away from our home ... all our possessions were left ... for Mother Nature to destroy ...," Bill Tcheripanoff Sr. of Akutan later recalled. "I tried to pretend it was really a dream and this could not happen to me and my dear family."

But it was no dream.

These evacuees were temporarily camped at the Wrangell Institute until they could be relocated to a Civilian Conservation Corps recreation camp at Ward Cove, near Ketchikan, and a cannery at Burnett Inlet, on Annette Island.

"For two weeks the Aleuts camped in Army tents on the school grounds. They were given three meals a day, primarily dog salmon, tea and bread," the wartime relocation commission report stated. "Men and women, young and old, were assigned chores in the Institute's kitchen, laundry and bakery. They also built a barge to transport lumber and other materials to Ward Lake.

"Army, Navy and civilian doctors examined the Aleuts; yet,

The balance of the evacuees from the Aleutian Islands stayed in tents in Wrangell for a few weeks before being assigned to other camps in Southeast Alaska.

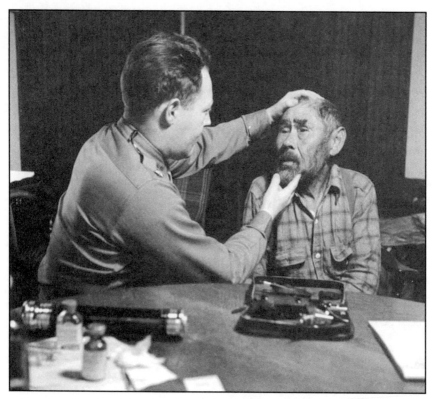

Military doctors examined the Aleut refugees when they arrived in Southeast Alaska.

according to one evacuee, they were not treated for tuberculosis, pneumonia, viruses or shock. Head lice were treated, however, and some children and adults were close-cropped, their scalps doused with kerosene to exterminate the parasites."

These Aleuts, who call themselves Unangan – which means "we the people" – then were taken to Ward Cove, located eight miles from Ketchikan. The camp, originally built in the 1930s to house no more than 70 people, had nine small cabins and four communal buildings.

Each cabin had a small kitchen and a bedroom with two bunk beds. The Aleuts built additional housing and furniture with lumber brought from Wrangell Institute and used scrap cardboard for insulation. Each household was issued a wood-burning stove, according to the commission report.

Right: An orthodox priest looks out the door of a cabin in a refugee camp in Southeast Alaska.

Below: A boy helps a young girl fill water from a community spigot in an Aleut refugee camp during World War II.

"Shared facilities for the nearly 200 evacuees included an out-house; a school; a church; and a laundry with a large tin basin, four cold-water faucets and two shower stalls," the report stated. "Water was hauled in buckets from an outside hydrant to each cabin, heated, then taken to the laundry. The village outhouse was a long open trough without seats, and insects were thick, despite the toilet's constant flow of water."

Unalaska's evacuees were moved to an abandoned cannery at Burnett Inlet on Etolin Island, where conditions were not as severe as the other camps.

Boys sit on lumber hauled ashore from Wrangell to build refugee housing for Aleuts relocated to Southeast Alaska in 1942.

CONFLICT IN THE ALEUTIANS

The cannery buildings were revamped, winterized and converted into small apartments. Four small houses, a school, teachers' quarters and a church also were built, the commission report stated. The death toll at this camp was lower than the others.

By the end of August 1942, a total of 881 Aleuts had been evacuated by the military from all villages west of Unimak Island, including the Pribilofs.

For the most part, the people hated the densely forested land of Southeast filled with stands of 150-foot spruce, cedar and hemlock. They were used to the windswept, treeless plains and beaches of the Aleutians where vegetation grew no taller than waist high.

"It was like being put in prison," Dorofey Chercasenn of Nikolski later told the commission. "My home was far away."

For most of the camps, school for the children and contact with the outside world was sparse. The evacuees lacked warm winter clothes, adequate diets and medicine to combat diseases that ran rampant.

The people suffered from influenza, measles, pneumonia and tuberculosis. Government records show that 32 died at Funter Bay, 17 at Killisnoo, 20 at Ward Cove and five at Burnett Inlet during their long ordeal.

Late in 1943, the U.S. government approved plans for the Aleuts to return to their homes following intense battles that drove the Japanese from the Aleutians. But even though Fish and Wildlife Service Director Ira Gabrielson was convinced that the Pribilof people should be returned to their homeland that September, the local agent in the Pribilofs said supplies and conditions were not suitable. He wrote a telegram to the assistant superintendent.

> "Whoever pushing fantastic idea rehabilitate Pribilofs not acquainted with conditions this time of year in Bering Sea. Landings here from now on very uncertain for any amount cargo work and for conveying women, children and sick people. Stop. Criminal charges should be preferred upon person responsible unless rehabilitation plans dropped for present until supplies and equipment obtained to properly equip station."

Pribilof Sealers Forced to Work

Drawn by the sound of roaring seals through a summer fog, Russian navigator Gavriil Pribilof discovered St. George Island in 1786. He found St. Paul Island, seen above, the next year.

The islands, teeming with fur seals, sea otters and sea lions, proved quite lucrative for the Russians after they found a workforce nearby in the Aleutian Islands.

Aleuts were forcibly taken to work as seasonal laborers in the fur seal harvest. By the 1820s, permanent settlements had been established on both St. George and St. Paul.

The Russians harvested the fur seals almost to extinction. So by 1847, they had adopted conservation methods for the harvesting and started taking 3- to 5-year-old non-breeding males. They did not kill any females.

The seal industry in the Pribilof Islands became a great moneymaker for the U.S. government following America's purchase of Alaska in 1867. And the evacuation of the Native seal hunters from the islands during World War II concerned many officials who wanted the revenue generated from the seal pelt sales to continue.

Secretary of the Interior Harold Ickes wrote to Secretary of War Henry Stimson in November 1942 and urged "that arrangements be made to return the natives and supervisory personnel ... to the Pribilof Islands next April or May to resume sealing and other operations."

Since many of the Pribilof sealers had entered the military, there were few men available to harvest seals that summer. But by May 1943, the U.S. Fish and Wildlife Service had received four-month furloughs for 17 draftees and deferments for four men not yet inducted so they could participate in the sealing season.

As the season drew nearer, Fish and Wildlife officials realized that some Aleuts did not want to return to the islands until the war was over, because they had good jobs in towns near their internment camps.

Superintendent Johnston decided to threaten the Natives in order to convince them to return to the Pribilofs.

"If any workman remains in Juneau or deserts his post during the summer ... [he] will forfeit any share of the sealing division. Also, I will seriously consider recommending that he be denied return to St. Paul for residence," Johnston said. "As St. George is being rehabilitated, any workman who refuses to return this spring will not share in the sealing division and will not be allowed to return at any later date if I can help it. This will include his immediate family (wife and children). Such a man will not receive assistance in any way from the Fish and Wildlife Service at any time and lose all privileges as an island resident."

Johnston's superiors told him that he did not have the power to make such threats.

CONFLICT IN THE ALEUTIANS

Upper left: Aleut workers club seals to death.

Lower left: Sealers strip the hides off dead seals.

Above: Workers salt seal pelts.

Right: Salted seal hides were slipped over boards in the tannery and processed.

But testimony before the wartime commission indicated that the Native men felt compelled to leave their jobs and return to the Pribilofs to harvest seals.

"They were told that if they did not, they would never see their homeland again," commission records show.

About 100 Aleuts harvested more than 117,000 seals — as evidenced by some of the carcasses seen above — during the summer of 1943. It was a record take that reaped more than $1.58 million in fur and seal by-product sales for the U.S. government.

The Aleuts received $1 per skin harvested, and the 13 non-Pribilof workers received $150 per month in salary.

Following the Alaska Native Claims Settlement Act of 1971, and pressure from animal rights groups, the U.S. government was out of the fur seal business by 1984.

The U.S. military was ready to protect Alaska's coastline, including manning camouflaged guns on the Pribilof Islands.

Evacuees returning in 1944 to St. George, seen above, were relieved to see their village had not been burned to the ground.

After drift ice no longer posed a danger, and the government acquired the necessary supplies and equipment, the people of the Pribilofs were transported from Funter Bay back to their islands in spring 1944.

The people of St. George found their village had not been destroyed as planned. But they did find broken windows and doors, ruined furniture and they discovered their religious icons had been taken.

Debate continued between the War Department, Navy, Army and other government officials regarding the return of the rest of the evacuees to the Aleutians. Finally a plan was agreed upon by May 1944, and funds allocated, but it wasn't implemented until 1945.

That April, a U.S. transport picked up people from Ward Cove, Burnett Inlet and Killisnoo and headed for the Aleutian Islands.

But upon their return, the evacuees found many of their villages had been ransacked. According to the wartime commission, the report on Unalaska was typical of the situation found on all the islands.

"All buildings were damaged due to lack of normal care and upkeep ... The furnishings, clothing and personal effects remaining in the homes showed, with few exceptions, evidence of weather damage and damage by rats. Inspection of contents revealed extensive evidence of widespread wanton destruction of property and vandalism. Contents of closed packing boxes, trunks and cupboards had been ransacked.

"Clothing had been scattered over floors, trampled and fouled. Dishes, furniture, stoves, radios, phonographs, books, and other items had been broken or damaged. Many items listed on inventories furnished by the occupants of the houses were entirely missing. ... It appears that armed forces personnel and civilians alike have been responsible for this vandalism and that it occurred over a period of many months."

Many Aleuts died during their internment, and some were buried in the Funter Bay cemetery, seen here.

Some evacuees returning to Atka lived in Quonset huts while they rebuilt their village.

Many Aleuts camped outdoors at first because their old homes had not yet been repaired. Many homes were uninhabitable.

The Army provided Unalaskans with 16- by 20-foot cabanas that had to be chained down due to 90 mph Aleutian winds.

Those living in Atka, where the village had been burned by the Navy, were given Quonset huts for shelter until the village could be rebuilt. As many as nine people lived in each hut in "conditions worse than the camps," according to the wartime commission.

But for the people of Biorka, Kashega and Makushin there would be no homecoming. Partly due to financial considerations, U.S. authorities decided these villages would be incorporated into the villages of Unalaska, Atka and Nikolski.

And the residents of Attu didn't get to go home, either. After spending the war in a Japanese concentration camp, the survivors returned to find that they had to coexist with their former enemies on Atka.

The evacuation of the people of the Aleutians and the Pribilofs changed their lives forever.

"Evacuation meant irreversible cultural erosion, destroying their means of pursuing a traditional subsistence way of life. They lost artifacts, but also the ability to recreate them. They lost (or found much reduced) the animals and sea creatures that had been essential to traditional subsistence," the wartime commission report said.

"The evacuation also destroyed many of the Aleuts' ties to their personal and religious pasts," the commission concluded. "America, proud of its cultural diversity, thereby lost a distinctive part of itself."

And for what? asked many of the evacuees.

"Some called the ordeal suffered by ... Aleut-Americans the 'craziness of war,' and dismissed that ugly portion of our history with that excuse," Agafon Krukoff Jr. of St. Paul said in a National Park Service article. "Not many of our people ... realized the ultimate insult of the entire story. The evacuations were not necessary; the Aleuts suffered for nothing."

Aleuts joined Japanese-Americans in the 1950s through 1980s in lawsuits to seek federal restitution for loss of property and civil liberties during their internment.

On Aug. 10, 1988, Public Law 100-383 was signed calling for financial compensation and an apology from Congress and the President. It granted reparations of $12,000 each to interned individuals still living, $1.4 million for damaged homes and churches, a $5 million trust for evacuees and descendants and $15 million to the Aleut Corp.

14

ENEMY OUSTED FROM ALEUTIANS

No enemy had occupied American soil since the War of 1812, until the Japanese went ashore at Kiska and Attu 130 years later. And in May 1943, Americans finally dislodged the enemy from its toehold on the westernmost tip of the Aleutians.

They did it in a battle that became – in proportion to the number of opposing troops – the second most costly war in the Pacific, second only to Iwo Jima. It was a battle that Secretary of War Frank Knox later described as the "most difficult and dangerous in all modern warfare."

The Aleutian campaign was building to a climax that spring when the U.S. infantry made the first amphibious island landing in its history.

About 15,000 troops began assembling at the beginning of May, four segments getting ready for the assault on the 40-mile island of Attu. One would be a reserve regiment, while the other three segments would hit Red Beach, Holtz Bay and Massacre Bay.

Massacre Bay, a sinister-sounding label, got its name when Russian fur traders slew 15 Aleuts there 200 years before. The American troops, perhaps whistling to keep up their courage, were already kidding about the name with such variations of their own as "Assassination Alley" and "Carnage Corner."

On May 11, 1943, U.S. troops headed for Attu Island in the military's first-ever amphibious landing. Cameramen who took photos of the landing at two points on the island, Massacre Bay and Holtz Bay, were under Japanese fire many times.

Here, heavily-laden landing boats, with soldiers crouching down out of line of sniper fire, approach the west arm of Holtz Bay.

Above: U.S. military landing boats were put over the sides of transports and moved toward the beach on Attu Island on May 11, 1943.

Below: The U.S. landing party was met by fierce fire from Japanese guns.

A detail of soldiers carry a wounded comrade across rough terrain on Attu Island, dodging sniper fire from the Japanese.

It lived up to its name. The Japanese lay in lines, holed in along the brow of the pass and along the ridges. They watched the Americans land, and soon heavy, accurate machine-gun fire came thundering down. Next day, the huge guns of the American battleship *Nevada* returned the fire, chewing great hunks out of the mountain. One observer wrote:

"Dead Japanese, hunks of artillery, pieces of guns and arms and legs rolled down out of the fog of the mountains."

Perhaps it was poetic justice that shells from the battleship did the damage, for the *Nevada* was one of the American ships damaged by the Japanese in the attack on Pearl Harbor. Now she was returning the compliment.

The Japanese commanded the U.S. positions on three sides, however, and in spite of the battleship's aid and help from aircraft, the

Above: U.S. soldiers lie against a berm as Japanese snipers attack them from the hills.

Below: American troops unpack shells and fire on the enemy during the battle of Attu.

Chaplain Ruben Curtis leads men in singing hymns at a burial service for U.S. soldiers killed in action at Massacre Bay on June 1, 1943. The cemetery is located in the valley about 2,000 yards from the northeast end of the beach. Each grave in the cemetery held eight bodies.

Americans made little headway in the early part of the campaign. By May 15, 56 Americans lay dead on the Aleutian island. There would be many more.

It was a tricky campaign; the island's terrain was almost as hard to conquer as the enemy, and the fog and mist and eternal raw chill took their toll as well as the enemy bullets. By the seventh day of battle, American troops had suffered 1,100 casualties, 500 of them from exposure. Before the battle was over, there would be 549 American and 2,351 Japanese dead.

A campaign that was expected to last a few days, stretched into weeks, and it wasn't until May 29 that the American pincers finally closed. On the night of May 30, a banzai charge of wildly yelling Japanese made a final effort.

Above: During the American drive on Chichagof Bay, U.S. forces came across groups of Japanese soldiers, 30 or 40 in a group. When the Japanese soldiers realized that they were trapped, they committed "hari-kari" with hand grenades held to their chests and heads.

Below: Only a few Japanese soldiers surrendered on Attu.

CONFLICT IN THE ALEUTIANS

U.S. soldiers raised the Stars and Stripes over an American post captured from the Japanese just inland from Holtz Bay. In the foreground, signalmen test their newly set up equipment. Other servicemen rest and start cooking fires, ready to enjoy a few moments of relaxation.

This warm fire on Attu's chilly beach on May 29, 1943, served a double purpose. It cooked a hot meal and thawed out the hands of U.S. soldiers.

When their attack failed, 500 men committed mass suicide by pulling the pins of their grenades and holding them against their chests and heads.

The U.S. military scoured the island for any remaining Japanese soldiers. They found several groups of dead enemy combatants in underground dwellings and caves that lined the hillsides.

The Japanese force suffered annihilation almost to the last man. Others held out in the hills and were not found until weeks later. When cornered, most chose death rather than capture. Only 28 prisoners were taken at Attu.

Once the island was secured, the military settled in to maintain control and then turned its attention to recapturing the island of Kiska.

Americans inspect a torn-up Aleutian battleground in this panoramic view of the Holtz Bay area of Attu, where strong Japanese installations were shelled and fought into submission by U. S. fighting men. A few enemy soldiers lived in underground dwellings and caves that dotted the cliffs.

Crates of supplies line the landscape of Attu as the American military built up to protect Alaska's shores.

On Aug. 15, 1943, the Allied invasion of Kiska began.

But there was no opposition to the 32,000 U.S. and Canadian forces because no Japanese troops were left on the island.

Under cover of fog, the Japanese fleet had secretly removed its 5,000 soldiers from Kiska by I-class submarines and surface vessels prior to the Allied attack.

Allied casualties during the invasion still numbered close to 200, however, as the enemy had set booby traps prior to leaving Kiska.

A mine in the harbor sunk a destroyer, killing 72 men. Another 17 Americans and four Canadians were killed from either booby traps or friendly fire, and 50 wounded. Trench foot infected about 130 men.

And following the battles for Attu and Kiska, hundreds of American servicemen would have their feet amputated as a result of frostbite and trench foot, an infection of the feet caused by cold, wet and insanitary conditions.

Above: American and Canadian troops land on a beach at Kiska in August 1943.

Left: Two American soldiers look out of a fortified underground trench on Kiska that previously had been occupied by Japanese soldiers.

One of the enemy prisoners captured, Kunio Sato, was among a party of 17 Japanese who visited the battleground at Attu in 1964 to conduct memorial services for the Japanese who died there.

They later came to Fort Richardson to bless the mass grave of 235 Japanese brought to the fort in 1953, cremated and buried en masse. A headstone bears the inscription, "Here Lies Unidentified Japanese Soldiers."

A second marker was erected by the visiting 1964 group, privately financed through a Japanese Buddhist organization. They erected a sacred four-sided marker, inscribed with Buddhist script, above their countrymen.

A few feet away from the Japanese dead are the graves of Russians and Canadians, most of whom had lost their lives ferrying war planes to our World War II allies. Across the road, a separate plot holds our American dead. Although their relatives may not find it possible to visit and honor the graves of these men buried far from home, their final resting place is peaceful and lovely with a backdrop of beautiful, white-capped mountains, and they are not forgotten. Although the suffering was theirs, the memory shall be ours.

Along with graves for American, Canadian and Russian soldiers who served and died during World War II, the original Fort Richardson was home to a mass grave for 235 unidentified Japanese soldiers.

15

1945: DISCRIMINATION TORPEDOED

As World War II drew to a close, Alaskans geared up to battle another enemy – discrimination.

Even though Alaska's Native people served with distinction guarding Alaska's borders, segregation thrived throughout the territory. Just like African-Americans in many of the contiguous United States, Alaska Natives had separate entrances, designated seating areas and different bathrooms than whites in public areas.

Discrimination against Alaska's Native people went on for years, as evidenced by the sign on this restaurant at the turn-of-the-last century.

Alberta Schenck fought against discrimination toward Alaska Natives in her hometown of Nome, seen here in 1946.

An incident in Nome during the mid-1940s put a spotlight on the situation. The Western Alaska gold-rush town boasted around 1,500 people, with Alaska Natives comprising about half that population.

On a cold winter evening in 1944 a lovely brunette with clear olive-colored skin walked into The Dreamland and sat with her date, a white U.S. Army sergeant.

Within minutes the movie theater's manager rushed to their seats. He told the girl to move to the "Native's only" section of the theater.

Her date told her to stay put.

The manager then called the chief of police, who arrived shortly thereafter and forcibly removed the young lady from the theater. He shoved her out into the bitter-cold arctic night and tossed her into jail.

Her crime?

Alberta Schenck had bucked the long-held status quo and dared to sit in the "white only" section of the theater. Although her father was Caucasian, a mixture of English and Irish, her mother was Native.

This young lady had a unique perspective on The Dreamland's dis-

The Nome Nugget

Published Monday, Wednesday and Friday by the
NOME PUBLISHING COMPANY
NOME, ALASKA
Telephone: Main 125 · P. O. Box 618

W. A. BOUCHER .... Editor-Publisher
EMILY BOUCHER .... Society Editor

2nd Class Application Made in Nome Post Office

FRIDAY, MARCH 3, 1944.

Communications

TO WHOM IT MAY CONCERN:
This is a long story, but will have to make it as brief as possible. It concerns race between natives, breeds and whites.

I believe we Americans and also our Allies are fighting for the purpose of freedom. Many of our early ancestors fought for the very same purpose, so their children and children's children, etc., would be free. I myself am part Eskimo and Irish and so are many others. I only truthfully know that I am one of God's children regardless of race, color, or creed. You or I or anyone else is not to blame what we are. But we are all proud to be what God has made us.

Why was it Thomas Jefferson and his men signed the Declaration of Independence? You or I know for certain that they did not fight and had thousands injured and killed for nothing. It has been known and said through centuries that all American citizens have the right to go, do and say what they please.

What has hurt us constantly is that we are not able to go to a public theater and sit where we wish, but yet we pay the SAME price as anyone else and our money is GLADLY received. We are not allowed even to go to public doings, only when money is concerned for the benefit of the so-called society people of our city.

These human beings who think they are in a higher standard than others admit they are citizens of America, but the majority are not loyal to what is written in the Constitution.

Every so often Red Cross donations are contributed by all the people regardless who they are, for the aid of foreign countries surrounding America. We gladly offer and give help to those in need but when Red Cross social entertainments are given, we are entirely left out. It looks as though we are not good enough to be invited.

Before war was declared ther ewere supposingly American people here in our city that were not even citizens of America. They evidently were the ones keeping us from attending social entertainments and complaining to where we should sit in a theater, because of being natives and part natives.

In other parts of Alaska all people are treated equally. Seemingly Nome is the only town in Alaska treating the natives and breeds as outcasts. These people trying to be so-called society people, are only following the steps of Hitlerism.

ALBERTA SCHENCK.

---

crimination practices. Alberta was an usher at the theater. But she was not allowed to show white people to their seats. Her job was to make sure that Natives stayed away from whites.

Alberta wrote about the injustices directed toward Alaska's Natives in an essay for her high school history class. It was published in the Nome Nugget newspaper.

"… I only truthfully know that I am one of God's children regardless of race, color, or creed. You or I or anyone else is not to blame what we are. But we are all proud to be what God has made us.

"… What has hurt us constantly is that we are not able to go to a public theater and sit where we wish, but yet we pay the same price as anyone else and our money is gladly received. We are not allowed even to go to public doings, only when money is concerned for the benefit of the so-called society people of our city."

Alberta's eviction from the

Alberta Schenck submitted an essay on discrimination to The Nome Nugget, which printed it on March 3, 1944.

theater sparked rebellion among Nome's residents, and U.S. Army Maj. Marvin "Muktuk" Marston recalled some of the events that followed in his book, "Men of the Tundra."

"… On my return (from a dog-mushing trip) the issue had reached white heat. On Sunday evening the Eskimos had lined up, bought their tickets and literally taken over the theater, sitting wherever they wanted to. They had filed charges against the theater manager and the chief of police. Feeling was at intense heat. The situation was critical — anything might happen."

Marston said Alberta and her family came to him seeking advice about legal counsel for a lawsuit. They were afraid that a white lawyer might not fight hard for their cause.

That's when the major got an idea that brought the issue to light for the territory's governor.

"… I asked Alberta to get me paper and pencil and proceeded to write out the simple facts of Alberta's forcible ejection from 'The Dreamland' and the subsequent developments. When finished, I handed it back to Alberta.

"'Now, Alberta, read this, and if it is a true and exact statement of the facts in the case, you sign it. Then when the telegraph office opens in the morning, you send this message to Governor (Ernest) Gruening at Juneau. If I am not mistaken, he will act at once.'"

According to Marston, the governor wired Nome Mayor Edward Anderson and asked about discrimination practices against Natives. He requested that the mayor investigate the matter involving Alberta and report back by wire.

A few hours later, the mayor sent the following message to the governor:

"A mistake has been made. It won't happen again."

But discrimination did not end.

Alaska's first people had been subjected to white men's dominance since the first Russian traders came in contact with them in the 1740s. And following the U.S. purchase of Alaska in 1867, Americans brought their prejudices north.

The 1867 Treaty of Cessions with the Russians declared that those living in Alaska "with the exception of uncivilized native tribes, shall be admitted to enjoyment of all the rights, advantages, and immunities of citizens of the United States. ..."

Thus Alaska's Natives were not deemed U.S. citizens.

"The uncivilized tribes will be subject to such laws and regulations as the United States may, from time to time, adopt in regard to aboriginal tribes of that country," the treaty declared.

As greed for gold and other resources took hold in the new American possession, the Mining Act passed in 1872 further shunned them. It stated that Alaska Natives were not permitted privileges afforded white miners as "... only U.S. citizens may claim land and loads, excluding Natives from their own properties."

Other injustices followed, including the mandatory use of English in all schools under the control of the Bureau of Indian Affairs. Children were punished if they spoke their native language.

Soon signs posted on businesses across Alaska voiced racial sentiments of the time: "No dogs, no Natives allowed."

The Alaska Native Brotherhood, organized by 12 Tlingit Natives from Southeast Alaska in 1912, began working toward changing perceptions about Alaska's Native people. Alaska Native Sisterhood organized a few years later.

Alaska Native Brotherhood founders, from left, are Paul Liberty, James Watson, Ralph Young, Eli Kalanvok (Katinook), Peter Simpson, Frank Mercer, James C. Jackson, Chester Worthington, George Fields, William Hobson (an early member) and Frank Price. Seward Kunz is not pictured.

Members of Alaska Native Sisterhood pose along a hillside in Douglas, Alaska, in 1921. Jimmie Fox, a Native leader, is seated in front of the group.

Both groups worked tirelessly to advocate for the civil rights of Alaska Natives, and eventually became powerful political forces in the territory.

In 1915, the Territorial Legislature created a way for Native people to become citizens of the United States. But it came with a heavy price.

The lawmakers said that citizenship would be granted to any Native who "severed all tribal relationships and adopted the habits of civilized life."

A Native needed to "wear Western clothing; not eat Indian foods or speak Indian languages; live apart from Indian village communities ..." in order to comply with the law.

And in addition to turning away from the traditional Native way of life, a Native needed the testimony of five white people that he or she had done so.

Nine years later, when the federal government passed a law permitting all American Indians and Alaska Natives to become full citizens, the Alaska Territorial Legislature passed a law requiring a literacy test so "illiterate Indians" couldn't vote. That law changed with the adoption of the Alaska Constitution in 1956.

Meanwhile, the Alaska Native Brotherhood and Sisterhood were becoming politically savvy in the white man's world. In 1924, the groups elected the first Native representative, William Paul Sr., to the Territorial Legislature. And beginning in 1929, they boycotted businesses that posted segregation signs.

The boycott partially succeeded, as most signs came down in Southeast Alaska. But they remained in other regions of the territory.

Two Native leaders, Elizabeth Peratrovich, grand vice president of the Alaska Native Sisterhood, and her

William Paul Sr. became the first Alaska Native to serve in the Territorial Legislature.

husband, grand president of the Alaska Native Brotherhood Roy Peratrovich, wrote to Gov. Gruening in 1941 about the "No Natives Allowed" sign hanging in the Douglas Inn near Juneau.

The governor already had persuaded some business owners and military leaders to take down segregation signs, but others refused. In response, Gruening submitted an act to the Territorial Legislature to outlaw the signs. Although the vote was close, it did not pass.

In the fall of 1944, following Alberta Schenck defying segregation in Nome, Frank Peratrovich and Andrew Hope, both Tlingits, won seats in the Territorial Legislature.

When the legislature met that winter, a law banning segregation signs again was atop the agenda. Alberta's story was among many testimonies about the treatment of Natives under widely accepted segregation practices in public spaces.

"Only an Indian can know how it feels to be discriminated against,"

Tlingit Frank Peratrovich was elected to the Alaska Territorial Legislature in 1944.

testified Roy Peratrovich during a Senate hearing on the equal rights issue on Feb. 6, 1945.

"Either you are for discrimination or you are against it," depending on how each legislator votes on this bill, he said.

Sen. Tolbert Scott argued that segregation worked well, and that only "mixed breeds" caused problems with segregation.

"It would have been far better had the Eskimos put up signs 'No Whites Allowed,'" Scott said. "… white women have done their part" to keep the races distinct, he continued. And he added that if white men had done as well, there would be no racial ill-feeling in Alaska.

Another argument heard against the bill during the hearing was that it would not end discrimination.

Following two hours of debate, Elizabeth Peratrovich testified. She told about the pain she felt when she was turned away from public places because she was Native, and the humiliation she suffered when ushered into "Natives only" areas.

She also reasoned with the legislative body that while a law might not eliminate discrimination, it could help curb it.

"Do your laws against larceny and even murder eliminate those crimes?" she asked. "No law will eliminate crimes but, at least, you as legislators, can assert to the world that you recognize the evil of the present situation and speak your intent to help us overcome discrimination."

The Anti-Discrimination Bill passed with vote of 11 to 5, and Gov. Gruening signed it into law on Feb. 16, 1945.

Born July 4, 1911, in Petersburg, Alaska, Elizabeth Wanamaker Peratrovich belonged to the Lukaax.adi clan of the Raven moiety - or tribe. Her parents died when she was young, and she was adopted.

She attended Petersburg Elementary School, Sheldon Jackson School, and graduated from Ketchikan High School. She continued her studies at Western College of Education in Bellingham, Wash.

Elizabeth, whose Tlingit name was Kaaxgal.aat, married Roy Peratrovich of Klawock on Dec. 15, 1931, in Bellingham. When the couple moved from Klawok to Juneau to raise their family in 1941, they were astonished to discover signs in business establishments revealing blatant discrimination against Alaska's Native people.

With the help of then-Territorial Gov. Ernest Gruening and Congressional Delegate Anthony J. Dimond, legislation was sponsored and introduced in the Territorial Legislature in 1943 to extend equal rights to Alaska's first people. But the bill was defeated.

It was introduced again during the winter of 1944-45.

As Grand Camp President of the Alaska Native Sisterhood, Elizabeth provided the crucial testimony that cultivated passage of the Anti-Discrimination Bill with a vote of 11-5.

Elizabeth died on Dec. 1, 1958, after a long battle with cancer. She is buried in Evergreen Cemetery in Juneau.

In 1988, the Alaska Legislature established Feb. 16 as the annual Elizabeth Peratrovich Day, the anniversary of the signing of the Anti-Discrimination Act.

SUPER RACE THEORY HIT IN HEARING

Native Sisterhood President Hits at "Rights" Bill Opposition

Opposition that had appeared to speak with a strong voice was forced to a defensive whisper at the close of yesterday's Senate hearing on the "Equal Rights" issue. Mrs. Roy Peratrovich, Grand President of the Alaska Native Sisterhood, the last speaker to testify, climaxed the hearing by wringing volleying applause from the galleries and Senate floor alike, with a biting condemnation of the "super race" attitude.

Reciting instances of discrimination suffered by herself and friends, she cried out against a condition that forces the finest of her race to associate with "white trash."

Answering the oft-voiced question, "will this law eliminate discrimination," Mrs. Peratrovich admitted that it would not; but, she queried in rebuttal, "do your laws against larceny and even murder prevent these crimes?" No law will eliminate crimes but, at least, you as legislators can assert to the world that you recognize the evil of the present situation and speak your intent to help us overcome discrimination, she said.

Opposition

Declaring their opposition to the law, unless it is amended, Senators Scott, Whaley, Collins and Shattuck spoke their feelings on the issue during the two hours of discussion; while Senators Walker and Cochran held forth in favor of the law. Senator Joe Green was chairman for the Committee of the Whole hearing.

Senator Allen Shattuck opened the discussion by repeating a statement he declared he had already made to Roy Peratrovich, Grand President of the Alaska Native Brotherhood. "This bill will aggravate, rather than allay, the little feeling that now exists," he stated. "Our native cultures have 10 centuries of white civilization to encompass in a few decades. I believe that considerable progress has already been made, particularly in the last 50 years." Senator Shattuck declared.

ANB President Talks

Peratrovich was then asked to the stand by Senator N. R. Walker and, following questions that established his education, background and right to speak for the Indians, Peratrovich was invited to express his views on the question before the Senate.

He pointed out that Gov. Ernest Gruening, in his report to the Secretary of the Interior, as well as in his message to the Legislature, had recognized the existence of discrimination. He quoted the plank adopted by the Democratic Party at its Fairbanks convention, which favored action on the natives' behalf. Reading the names of the members of the committee that helped to frame that plank, he pointed out that among them were members of the present Senate body.

"Only an Indian can know how it feels to be discriminated against," Peratrovich said. "Either you are for discrimination or you are against it," accordingly as you vote on this bill, he added.

Has Amendment

Declaring that he had an amendment to propose to the measure, Senator Frank Whaley read a lengthy prepared address to the assembly, in which he labelled the measure a "lawyer's dream" and a "natural in creating hard feeling between the whites and natives." He stated his flying experience in many parts of Alaska as authority behind the opinion he had reached. Declaring himself "personally assailed" by Senator Whaley in his remarks, Senator O. D. Cochran raised his voice for the bill, offering instances of discrimination which came, he declared, from a list of similar occurrences in his own knowledge that would occupy the full afternoon to relate. As in his speech on the matter before the House, Senator Cochran made use of a theatre in Nome as a prime example of an establishment where discrimination is practiced. Senator Walker supported Senator Cochran's views, declaring that he knew no instance where a native had died from a broken heart, but adding that he did know of situations where discrimination had forced Indian women into living lives "worse than death."

Scott Talks

Senator Tolbert Scott, in one of his rare participations in debate, spoke from the heart, his feeling that the bill, as it stood, would not accomplish the purpose intended. "Mixed breeds," he declared, are the source of the trouble. It is they only who wish to associate with the whites. "It would have been far better had the Eskimos put up signs 'No Whites Allowed'," he said. He stated his belief that the issues was being raised to create political capital for some legislators, and concluded that white women have done their part in keeping the races distinct; if white men had done as well, there would be no racial feeling in Alaska.

Liquor Problem

Speaking from his long experience, among the Eskimo peoples in particular, Senator Grenold Collins furnished a sincere and authoritative voice in opposition to the bill. He supported Senator Scott's contention regarding mixed breeds by citing the well-being of the Eskimos of St. Lawrence Island, where white men have not worked their evil. "Eskimos are not an inferior race," he stated, "but they are an individual race." The pure Eskimos are proud of their origin and are aware that harm comes to them from mixing with whites. It is the mixed breed who is not accepted by either race who causes the trouble. Declaring, "I believe in racial pride" and do not think this bill will do other than arouse bitterness, Senator Collins lashed out at the sale of liquor to natives, as the root of trouble.

A motion to report progress, offered by Senator Walker, was approved, following the testimony of Mrs. Peratrovich, which terminated discussion.

Ill, Bill! Its' Feb. 7

The Daily Alaska Empire in Juneau reported on Elizabeth Peratrovich's powerful testimony during a Territorial Legislature hearing on discrimination.

Territorial Gov. Ernest Gruening signs the Anti-Discrimination Bill, which was passed in the spring of 1945. Surrounding him are, from left, Sen. O.D. Cochran, D-Nome; Elizabeth Peratrovich of Klawock; Rep. Anderson, D-Klawock; Sen. N.R. Walker, D-Ketchikan; and Roy Peratrovich, D-Klawock.

But as offensive signs of segregation came down, Alaska Natives continued to encounter prejudice in other areas.

Covenant restriction policies for Airport Heights subdivision, built in Anchorage in 1948, excluded all non-whites from owning property in the area. And when Turnagain Heights Subdivision was built in 1953, its covenants denied ownership or renting to non-whites – unless they were servants for white people.

One of the last barriers of discrimination against Natives disintegrated in 1976 when Alaska Natives won the right to have schools built in their communities. Prior to what has become known as the Molly Hootch case, children had to leave their villages and travel to boarding schools to continue their education past the eighth grade.

16

1947: REEVE AIRWAYS TAKES FLIGHT

One of Alaska's most respected bush pilots launched his own airline with a 21-passenger Douglas DC-3 C-47 Skytrain Dakota purchased from the U.S. Air Force in March 1947. Robert "Bob" Campbell Reeve birthed Reeve Aleutian Airways Inc. to serve the people of the Aleutian Chain.

Reeve, who landed in Alaska as a stowaway on board a steamship in 1932, started out with only a few cents in his pocket. A chance encounter with Valdez aviator Owen Meals started Reeve down his long and distinguished career in Alaska's skies.

Robert Reeve, seen here atop a plane, began repairing airplanes in Valdez when he arrived in 1932. The other men in the photo are Owen Meals, right, and an unidentified man.

Robert Reeve used this primitive hangar in his early operations in Valdez.

Meals had just crashed his single-engine Eaglerock biplane and Reeve, one of the nation's first certified airplane mechanics, repaired it. Reeve then leased the plane, cleared an airstrip in a cow pasture and began a charter business.

Reeve spent the next 15 years flying as a bush pilot around the Great Land and building quite a reputation with his daring antics before he formed his airline. He pioneered new flight routes to get to hard-to-reach mines, developed a method for landing on mud flats with skis and set down on many glaciers and ice fields. His 2,000-some glacier landings earned him the nickname "Glacier Pilot."

Along with his twin brother, Richard, Robert was born in Waunake, Wis., on March 27, 1902 – a year before Orville Wright's successful 12-second sustained flight in Kitty Hawk, N.C.

"The weather was so bad the year that I was born not one plane got off the ground," he often joked.

Robert Reeve became enthralled with flying and read all he could on the subject.

By age 15, wanderlust took over and he enlisted in the U.S. Army. He saw his first airplanes when a few Curtiss JN-4 Jennies flew over

Fort Benjamin Harrison in Indiana. And while stationed at Camp Custer in Michigan, he paid $5 to ride in an airplane for five minutes.

That five minutes changed his life. Aviation entered his blood.

Before coming to Alaska, Reeve, who earned his commercial pilot's license in 1926, had flown for barnstormers in Texas and delivered airmail in South America. He set a speed record on a flight betwéen Santiago, Chili, and Lima, Peru, according to "Flying Beats Work: The Story of Reeve Aleutian Airways," by Stan Cohen. Reeve, who only used a compass during the night flight, covered 1,900 miles in 20 hours at an altitude that never exceeded 100 feet.

He also flew a Fairchild 71 over the Andes at altitudes exceeding 23,000 feet without oxygen while on a route between Santiago and Montevideo, Uruguay.

"It was the best performer at high altitudes of any airplane I have ever flown," Reeve later recalled of the Fairchild.

While in South America, he heard tales about Alaska that enticed him north. Following a short visit in the states, and a bout with polio

that bothered one leg for years, he stowed away on a steamer and arrived in Anchorage.

But there were too many pilots in town, so he ended up in Valdez.

By the winter of 1932, he'd earned enough money to buy his first plane, a Fairchild 51. Four years later, he bought a Fairchild 71.

The pioneer aviator married Janice Morisette in 1936, and the following year, the

Robert Reeve, seen here on his first airplane – a Fairchild 51 – developed a way to land on mud flats using skis.

couple welcomed the first of their five children – Richard.

That year also brought one of Reeve's last glacier landings.

While ferrying the Washburn Expedition of 1937 to Mount Lucania in Canada, Reeve landed on a glacier at an altitude of 8,750 feet – more than 1,800 feet higher than any other plane had landed with passengers and freight, according to Cohen. Due to an unusually warm winter, much snow had melted, and the plane sunk belly-deep in the slush.

Reeve waited a week for the weather to cool so he could take off.

Robert and Janice Reeve pose in front of an airplane in 1937.

"Ahead of me I could see the big crevasses – if I hit one of them I was a goner," Reeve recounted in Cohen's book. "I happened to glance left and spotted a smooth icefall with about a 500-foot drop-off. I made a sharp turn and dove right over the wall ... We sailed into the air, about 10 feet from the bottom."

When the engine on the airplane quit the next day, Reeve decided its flying days were over, and he never flew it again.

The following year marked a string of bad luck for the young aviator.

His twin died in a plane crash in 1938. The next spring brought a fierce windstorm that flipped his remaining airplane. And just after he had repaired it, a fire in the hangar destroyed it.

The Reeve family moved to Fairbanks in 1941, and then to

Robert Reeve, above, racked up around 2,000 landings on glaciers.

Anchorage the next year. Reeve began flying personnel and materials for the Alaska Communication System. As the only bush pilot under exclusive contract with the military, Reeve winged his way across mainland Alaska, the Aleutians and Western Canada.

As he learned about the Aleutian weather, islands and coastlines, he formed a plan to serve the 1,783-mile Aleutian route with scheduled air service.

Following the end of World War II, Reeve bought a surplus DC-3 C-47 from the Air Force and converted it for civilian use. His fledgling business took off following a steamship strike. He and his two pilots made 26 roundtrip flights between either Anchorage or Fairbanks and Seattle in 53 days. The money earned from those flights helped pay off his loan for the first surplus plane and financed another three DC-3s.

With safety a major concern, Reeve created a checklist for his pilots. And when he missed one of the items on the list in 1948, he fired himself and let his license expire, according to Cohen.

The bush pilot's airline grew during the 1950s and 1960s as it acquired leases to many old military airfields down the Aleutian Chain. Soon DC-3s, DC-4s and many other types of aircraft were added to the fleet and moving construction workers and supplies to new

This advertisement appeared in the September 1953 issue of The Alaska Sportsman.

Reeve Aleutian Airways transported many tuberculosis patients to medical care facilities.

Robert "Bob" Campbell Reeve signed his portrait with "Best Wishes to the Cook Inlet Historical Society."

Distant Early Warning System sites.

Fire again played havoc on the business in 1964 when a blaze destroyed the company's administrative offices in Anchorage. And just as the business was getting back on its feet in 1975, fire in a hangar burned two airplanes.

Robert Reeve, named Alaskan of the Year in 1972 and inducted into the National Aviation Hall of Fame in 1975, stepped down as the CEO of the company in 1978. He turned the helm over to his son, Richard, who propelled the family business into the jet age. Two Boeing 727s were added to the Aleutian fleet and served with distinction until the company had to call it quits in 2001. Competition and deregulation of the airline industry sealed the end for the nearly 60-year-old company.

The Glacier Pilot died in his sleep on Aug. 25, 1980, and was inducted into the Alaska Aviation Pioneer Hall of Fame on Feb. 25, 2005.

A model of Reeve's first airplane, along with his flight goggles and cap, are on display at the Valdez Museum.

17

1948: Murderer Nominated King

T he Anchorage Fur Rendezvous, which was temporarily suspended during World War II, resumed again with a flourish in 1946 and began drawing visitors from Fairbanks, Juneau and Seattle. Several events were added to the annual winter festival, including the Miners & Trappers Ball, Melodrama and the World Championship Sled Dog Race. A large fireworks display was added to the opening-night ceremonies the following year that coincided with the crowning of the Rondy Queen.

And in 1948, another first was ushered in when one of the community's most colorful characters, Jacob Marunenko, was nominated for Mardi Gras King. Known as Russian Jack, this homesteader also was a murderer.

Marunenko had left a wife and two small children in the Ukrainian village of Parevka in the early 1900s when he headed to the Last Frontier. Naturalization papers on file at the National Archives show that Marunenko traveled on a Canadian Pacific Railway train south from Canada in May 1915, entering the United States at Blaine, Wash.

By 1920, he was well-entrenched in the new railroad town at Ship Creek and had changed his name to Jack Marchin. Census records show he owned the Montana Pool Room at 435 Fourth Avenue, as well as a cabin, and could read and write.

Russian Jack owned the Montana Pool Room, seen here on the left side of Fourth Avenue in 1915.

Marchin's whereabouts between the mid-1920s and 1930s are sketchy, but when the Alaska Railroad was finally finished in 1923, many European-born construction workers drifted off to find work elsewhere.

Anchorage went dormant for a while, serving as a shopping center for outlying mining operations and getting by on the generosity of the federal government. According to Z.J. Loussac Public Library historian Bruce Merrell, civilization came in fits and starts: flower gardens replaced stump-filled yards, wood-stave water mains for a sewer system replaced outhouses and a larger school replaced the old Pioneer Schoolhouse.

During the 1920s and 1930s several of Anchorage's future prominent citizens moved to town. Another Russian immigrant named Z.J. "Zack" Loussac relocated from Iditarod and started a drug store that made him wealthy beyond his dreams; John and Marie Bagoy built a greenhouse that supplied the community with fresh-cut flowers and vegetables; and a young reporter named Robert Atwood arrived from Illinois, married the banker's daughter, Evangeline Rasmuson, and took over as editor of the Anchorage Daily Times.

Then Marchin pops back into the scene, earning a living doing carpentry and hauling wood. He also earned money making moonshine in an illegal still on his homestead property, about three miles east of the city center, and hauling it to town by wagon.

Russian Jack made a living by selling moonshine to Anchorage residents.

The bootlegging entrepreneur made regular deliveries to "the girls on the line," as well as to several of the town's more prominent citizens. He earned a pretty good living running his business from his homestead during the summer and out of a house between A Street and Barrow Street off Fifth Avenue during the winter.

But on March 22, 1937, he attended a drinking party that erupted into violence and left one man dead.

Marchin, who admitted to shooting taxi driver Milton Hamilton during the drinking party at a cabin on Fifth Avenue in March 1937, made headlines for the Anchorage Daily Times on Jan. 21, 1938: "'Russian Jack' Marchin Tells His Story.'"

In his account of events during his trial, Russian Jack explained that he shot Hamilton while being choked:

"The defendant, wearing a leather jacket, breeches and high shoe-pacs, appeared calm as he told the jury his story of events leading up to the shooting, and pointed out injuries he said he sustained when he was attacked by Hamilton in the cabin of Mrs. Doris Simmons on East Fifth Avenue.

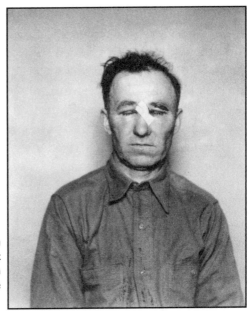

This mug shot of Russian Jack, taken by the Anchorage Police Department following a fatal shooting on March 22, 1937, shows he was on the receiving end of a few punches.

The Anchorage Daily Times, pictured below in 1957, reported the events that unfolded during Russian Jack's trial for murder.

"Russian Jack admitted firing the shot that sent a bullet through Hamilton's brain and killed him instantly. But he testified that he had no intention of killing the man. ...

"Marchin, a man of medium size weighing 155 pounds and gracing a flowing mustache, described the events preceding the shooting:

"'During the afternoon of March 21, I worked in the woods. I walked six miles into the woods to work and took my gun for protection from wolves and coyotes. I carried the gun in the pocket of my coat.'"

Marchin said he'd then been invited to Simmons' home for a party with her and her brothers. After hours of drinking beer and wine, Milton Hamilton and others joined them.

Russian Jack said he took along a gun to protect himself from wolves when he went into the woods the day of the fatal shooting incident.

"'I had heard that Hamilton was strong and rough. I was afraid of him. I stayed in the bedroom all evening after Hamilton arrived.

"'Later I went into the kitchen. Hamilton was on a chair near the stove. He walked across the kitchen and started beating me. He had a big ring on a finger and it cut my face. I had a cut on the forehead, my nose was broken, both my eyes were blackened. He broke two of my teeth.'"

Russian Jack then explained that he didn't want to bleed all over Simmons' house, so he stepped outside. When he realized he'd forgotten his coat, he went back inside to fetch it.

"'Someone grabbed me by the throat and started choking and beating me. I tried to holler but couldn't because of the choking. Something hit me hard on the head. I was afraid I was going to be killed.

"'I remembered my gun. I couldn't get away. I got the gun from the coat pocket and shot once to make a noise and get loose. I didn't know which way I shot.'"

An Anchorage jury found Russian Jack guilty of manslaughter in the death of cab driver Milton Hamilton, who may have driven a taxi similar to this 1937 Dodge.

The jury found Marchin not guilty of first-degree murder, but guilty of manslaughter and recommended leniency. Judge Simon Hellenthal sentenced Marchin to 2-1/2 years in the federal penitentiary at McNeil Island, Wash.

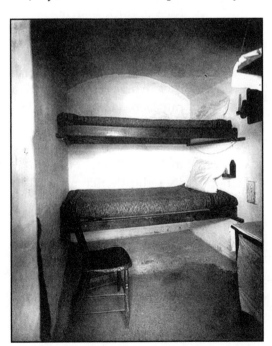

Russian Jack Marchin returned to Anchorage after serving a portion of his sentence. By the late 1940s, it seems that most of Anchorage had forgotten or forgiven him for his transgression because Marchin was nominated for an auspicious post during the 1948 Fur Rendezvous.

Following his conviction for manslaughter, Russian Jack spent some time locked up in a cell, similar to this one, at McNeil Island Penitentiary in Washington state.

HEAR YE! HEAR YE!
LET'S ELECT
"RUSSIAN JACK"

For **MARDI GRAS**
K I N G

To elect "RUSSIAN JACK" is a crowning glory to
Crowning Event of the season!

CITY MIKE'S HOTEL AND COCKTAIL BAR
NORTH STAR LIQUOR STORE
OK BARBER SHOP

This ad encouraging Anchorage residents to vote for Russian Jack for Mardi Gras King appeared in the Anchorage Daily Times in 1948.

A large ad appeared in the Anchorage Daily Times that urged readers to vote for Russian Jack as "Mardi Gras King."

The Mardi Gras Ball was held at the Aleutian Gardens night club. More than 50 prizes for best costumes and "Beautiful Girls in the Sensational Arctic Strip Tease" highlighted the event.

City Mike's Hotel and Cocktail Bar, along with the North Star Liquor Store and the OK Barber Shop, backed Russian Jack Marchin's candidacy for king. Marchin looked quite dapper at the festivities, sporting slicked back hair, waxed handlebar mustache and wearing a coat and tie.

Marchin lost the election to Kurly Braga, but he was named prince of the events. His popularity indicates that most of the community felt Marchin had paid his debt to society and welcomed him back.

One Anchorage resident told historian Merrell that Hamilton "deserved being killed anyway."

Since Marchin wasn't a U.S. citizen, he put his "homestead" under the names of his best friend, Peter Toloff, and Nicholas Darlopaulos. However, unable to "prove up," they lost the land back to the federal government in 1943. That was around the time the Anchorage City

Council was investigating the freshwater spring on the parcel as a potential source for drinking water for the community.

In 1948, the city got title to the 320-acre piece of property, and today it is a popular sanctuary, golf course and ski trail site known as Russian Jack Springs Park.

Russian Jack Marchin became a naturalized citizen of the United States in 1954 and signed both his names on this photograph.

Marchin became a naturalized citizen in 1954, at the age of 70, and moved to California sometime after 1959, perhaps at the request of a lady friend. He relocated for the last time in 1967 to the small town of Arvin, Calif., some 50 miles out in the desert from Bakersfield, where he lived out the rest of his life.

He died of heart disease on Oct. 28, 1971, shortly after turning 88, and was buried in the Arvin Cemetery. A few years ago, Anchorage pioneer and late Alaska historian John Bagoy arranged for a headstone to mark his grave.

Russian Jack is still very much alive in the city of Anchorage, however. The bootlegger-homesteader-murderer has a street, a large park, a bank branch, an apartment complex, a post office and even an elementary school named after him.

Special thanks to Anchorage Z.J. Loussac Public Library historian and bibliographer Bruce Merrell, who provided research used to compile this story.

18

1948: ALASKA AIRLINES MAKES HISTORY

A laska Airlines flew into the history books when, in 1948, it participated in the Berlin Airlift. The frontier airline, built slowly during several decades, was by that time reportedly the largest charter airline in the world.

Its journey to that status began in the early 1930s.

"Alaska is an airline built from humble beginnings in 1932 by a cast of always dedicated, sometimes quirky and often brilliant characters," wrote aviation historian Robert J. Serling, author of "Characters & Characters, The Spirit of Alaska Airlines."

The first in the long line of characters that fill the pages of Alaska Airlines' history was fur trader Linious "Mac" McGee. Along with reputedly hard-drinking bush pilot Harvey "Barney" Barnhill, he bought a three-seat Stinson in 1931 for $5,000 in San Francisco. McGee, who planned to use the airplane in his fur-trading business, flew the plane to Seattle, then dismantled it and shipped the craft north by steamer to Valdez, according to an article in Business Wire magazine in May 2001. When it arrived, McGee had it reassembled and flown to Anchorage. The next year he advertised in the Anchorage Daily Times that McGee Airways also offered charter service between Anchorage and Bristol Bay.

"Fly an Hour or Walk a Week," the ad stated.

McGee, who had stowed away on an Alaska-bound steamship

Alaska Airlines traces its roots to McGee Airways, established by Linious "Mac" McGee and Harvey "Barney" Barnhill in 1932.

during the Great Depression in 1929, and Barnhill bought a second Stinson early in 1932. But the men split ways that spring, according to the Alaska Airlines Web site.

Although McGee knew how to fly, he preferred to manage the company. So he hired another airman, Oscar Winchell, to handle the flying. Winchell, a cowboy turned bush pilot, became known as the Flying Cowboy, wrote author Geza Szurovy in "Bushplanes."

Later that year, McGee bought the second Stinson from Barnhill. He then hired more pilots and pioneered the concept of building a fleet of identical airplanes so the parts would be interchangeable. He paid his pilots 12.5 percent of the take from flights they generated, according to Szurovy.

By the mid-1930s, McGee started focusing on the mining industry, according to an article titled "Alaska Airlines 75th Anniversary" by Jim Glab, published in Air Transport World in December 2007. McGee decided to sell his airline to another charter business, Star Air Service, in 1934.

Seattle fliers Charlie Ruttan, Steve Mills and Jack Waterworth founded Star Air Service in April 1932 with financial backing from Earl Dunkle, a wealthy Alaskan mining engineer. The Anchorage-based pilots bought a single-engine, two-seat Fleet biplane to open a flight school. But since the training business was slow, they branched out into charters.

Disaster struck that Fourth of July when the aviation adventurers took a job for $100 to fly over an Independence Day crowd. The black powder used to make a smoke trail damaged the plane's wings.

Another pilot crashed the plane soon after the aviators had repaired the damage, so the men had to get other jobs to make the money necessary to fix it.

An investor helped pay for a Curtiss Robin soon after the biplane was airworthy again, making Star a two-plane operation. The Curtiss, with its enclosed cabin, allowed the little airline to operate during the winter. It then started getting contracts to haul airmail and bought a few more planes for the growing business.

When the flyboys bought McGee Airways – and added its seven silver-and-black Stinsons to the company's inventory – their 15-plane fleet became the largest airline in Alaska, according to Glab.

Bush planes carried all sorts of supplies throughout remote Alaska. These reindeer in Naknek, located in Bristol Bay, await a boarding call for Star Airways during the 1930s.

But Star Airways had problems making payments on its $50,000 purchase, so McGee bought his way back into the business and took over management of the airline. He bought out Waterworth in 1936, after Mills died in a plane crash, and later the struggling Alaska Interior Airlines, founded by Winchell.

After McGee's last partner, Ruttan, left the airline in late 1937, McGee sold the company to a corporation that included one of his former pilots, Don Goodman. The group changed the name to Star Air Lines.

By this time, the motley collection of planes included a Ford Tri-motor, a Fairchild Pilgrim and several Bellancas, according to Glab.

But the company was becoming more professional. Along with establishing radio stations along the lower Kuskokwim and Yukon rivers to support its Southwest operation, it also chose corporate colors and painted its planes in black and orange.

When the corporation sold the airlines to wealthy New York wheeler-dealer R.W. Marshall in 1942, the new owner changed the name again and it became Alaska Star Airlines. Two years later, he dropped the middle name.

Marshall was known for questionable business practices and not paying his bills, according to Glab. So morale within the new company was low.

"Pilots often had to pay for fuel out of their own pockets and the company was the target of frequent lawsuits," Glab wrote.

By the end of World War II, Marshall placed a new manager at the helm.

James Wooten, who had made a name for himself by launching an air cargo business for American Airlines, brought energy and new ideas to Alaska Airlines. He aggressively sought charters to carry cargo and passengers across the globe. His efforts landed the company a lucrative deal during the Berlin Airlift to ferry tons of lifesaving supplies into Berlin after the Soviet Union blocked all rail and road access to the German city.

Following World War II, Germany was divided between America, Great Britain, France and the Soviet Union. These one-time allies, representing opposing economic structures of capitalism and communism, were to run their sectors by military government until a suitable national government could be created that would put the country back together.

The United States, England and France combined their zones and called the military province Trizone. The Soviets, who hoped to continue the German recession, did not want to be part of the plan to unify the country. The Russians refused to endorse or use the unified currency that the three-

Alaska Airlines charter flights helped deliver much-needed supplies to Berlin, seen here in the mid-1940s, during the Soviet Union's 1948 blockade.

some had created on June 18, 1948, to promote economic stability.

On June 24, in a move to push the West out, Soviet leader Joseph Stalin halted all traffic into and out of the Russian section of Berlin at Marienborn, 100 miles away from the city.

Stalin thought a disgruntled German populace would rise up and embrace communism if he played his cards right, according to documents in the Harry S. Truman Library.

Those living in the beleaguered city soon were desperate for food, medicine and other necessities.

Western reaction was swift.

"The place to mark a stand against Russia is right here in Berlin," said Maj. Gen. William J. "Wild Bill" Donovan, wartime director of the Office of Strategic Services. "This is not a cold war. It is hot as hell. ..."

Alaska Airlines purchased surplus military planes, like this C-46, following World War II.

Alaska Airlines, which after the war had moved its corporate offices to Seattle and acquired a fleet of surplus military aircraft that included DC-3, DC-4 and C-46 transports, joined the airlift that carried more than 2 million tons of supplies in 270,000 flights.

The Russians ended their blockade in May 1949.

Shortly thereafter, the Alaskan air carrier again flew onto the world stage as it ferried thousands of Jews to Israel.

The government of Israel, established in 1947 when the United Nations passed a resolution to partition Palestine, mounted airlift operations in 1949 to bring Jewish people to the new country after the Imam of Yemen agreed to let 45,000 Jews leave his country.

Operating on a charter basis, Alaska Airlines joined other carriers and shuttled Jews from Aden, the capital of Yemen, to their new homeland. The airlines modified C-46 aircraft to shuttle 76 passengers and 60-passenger DC-4s to carry 150 people, the Alaska Airlines Web site said. The company also painted an eagle with outstretched wings over the door of each plane used in the mission.

"Their legend said they would be returned to Israel on the wings of an eagle," said Alaska Airlines pilot and mechanic Stanley Epstein, who ferried people during this humanitarian effort. "... it reassured people when they got on the plane."

Alaska Airlines carried up to 150 people per trip during Opertion Magic Carpet.

"One of the things that really got to me was when we were unloading a plane at Tel Aviv," said Marian Metzger, a flight attendant who assisted Israeli nurses on a number of flights. "A little old lady came up to me and took the hem of my jacket and kissed it. She was giving me a blessing for getting them home. We were the wings of eagles."

Epstien said the operation was fraught with danger, but only one plane was forced to land in enemy territory.

"... it ran out of fuel and landed in Port Sudan (Egypt). The pilot (Bob Maguire) told the airport officials he needed ambulances right away to take his sick passengers to the hospital," Epstien said. "They asked why, and he told them the passengers had smallpox. They wanted him out of there right away so he got some fuel and left."

To avoid being shot down by militant Arabs, Operation Magic Carpet pilots flew a circuitous route through Africa, often facing 16-hour days as they covered almost 3,000 miles one way.

Alaska Airlines, other carriers and the military ferried more than 40,000 people to Israel during the secret mission that flew between December 1948 and early 1950.

The media was informed of the operation, which had no fatal accidents, several months after its completion.

Alaska Airlines won temporary federal permission for its first scheduled route linking Seattle, Portland, Ore., Fairbanks and Juneau in the early 1950s. The approval became permanent in 1957.

The airlines continued to grow, introducing its first jetliner, a Convair 880, in 1961 and its first Boeing 727s shortly thereafter. It acquired several small airlines in 1968, including Ellis Airlines, Alaska Coastal Airlines and Cordova Air.

In 1968, Alaska Airlines acquired several small carriers based in Southeast Alaska, including Ellis Airlines.

Robert "Bob" Ellis, seen here on his floatplane in Sitka in 1937, began his flying business in 1936 with a four-seat, single-engine Cabin Waco floatplane in Ketchikan. He called his new venture Ellis Air Transport, but later renamed it Ellis Airlines.

Following World War II, he added surplus Grumman Goose aircraft to his fleet and joined forces with Alaska Coastal Airlines, a Juneau-based carrier operated by aviation pioneers Shell Simmons and Ben Benecke in 1962. The company became part of Alaska Airlines six years later.

"Bob was a true pioneer, instrumental in developing aviation in the state of Alaska and helping make Alaska Airlines a success," according to the airline's Web site. "He was a warm person with a ready smile and a good story to tell."

An Ellis Air Transport floatplane sits near a watery hangar in 1939.

Prior to hooking up with Ellis Airlines, and later Alaska Airlines, Shell Simmons had been busy building his Alaska Coastal Airlines business, seen above, in Juneau and making a name for himself taking on heroic rescues and mercy missions. Known for his daring exploits, he also was known as someone who put "no stock in heroism ... he just did what he thought was right," according to Alaska Airlines' Web site.

Simmons, who first came to Alaska as a teen, caught the flying bug while working on a runway project in the Arctic. He watched in fascination as fliers like Noel Wien landed on the unfinished airstrip.

He learned to fly in Yakima Valley, Wash., in 1929, and then returned north to work at the Alaska-Juneau mine. That's where he began working on airplanes and honing his flying skills.

In 1934, he started flying for a local carrier. But when his plane was damaged during a storm, and his employers couldn't afford to have it repaired, Simmons bought the wreck for $1. He then found some investors and began Alaska Air Transport.

Five years later, he joined with Alex Holden of Marine Airways to create Alaska Coastal Airways. And in 1962, that company merged with Ketchikan-based Ellis Airlines to become the largest scheduled airline exclusively operating amphibians.

The company then merged with Alaska Airlines in 1968.

Alaska Airlines also acquired Cordova Airlines and its fleet, one of which is seen here, in 1968.

The story of the airline, based in Cordova along Prince William Sound in Southcentral Alaska, began in 1934 when Kirk Kirpatrick started the flying service and a repair shop on Eyak Lake airstrip.

Kirkpatrick hired a daring Midwestern barnstormer, Merle "Mudhole" Smith, in 1937. Smith had earned his nickname on one of his first flights, a trip to a mine near McCarthy.

Robert Reeve, one of Alaska's most famous aviators, usually made the run to the Bremner Mine in the winter when the ground was hard enough to land. But on this particular trip, Smith was at the controls when he landed the Cordova Air Services biplane on soggy ground during the summer.

The plane's tailskid knocked a rock out of place and made a hole in the ground. Later, upon takeoff following a rain, one of the plane's wheels went into the hole and made the plane take a nose dive. Smith spent the evening cleaning the mud out of the plane's engine, using a screwdriver, putty knife and a rag.

When Reeve learned of the incident, he tagged Smith with the name Mudhole, by which he was known the rest of his life.

Following Kirkpatrick's death in 1939, Smith became president of the now-named Cordova Airlines. He eventually bought out the other directors. After the merger with Alaska Airlines in 1968, Smith continued to operate a charter business, Chitina Air Service.

19

In Other News ...

1940: Sydney Laurence Dies

Among the memorials in the Anchorage Municipal Park Cemetery stands a small, pink marker adorned with a palette. It is the final resting place of Sydney Mortimer Laurence, one of Alaska's greatest artists.

Known for his dramatic landscape paintings, Laurence was one of the first profession-ally trained artists to live in the territory. His works, which often featured Mt. McKinley, hang in the Musee du Louvre in Paris, the National Art Gallery in Washington, D.C., and many other locations around the world.

Laurence, born in Brooklyn, N.Y., on Oct. 14, 1865, first came north in search of gold in the early 1900s. Correspondence from his first wife, Alexandria Fredericka Dupre, and two young sons, indicate he was somewhere around Tyonek on the northwest shore of Cook Inlet, according to the Sydney Laurence Web site. The then-38-year-old didn't paint much in those first years, but prospected in the summer and earned a living as a photographer in the winter.

He moved to the new town of Anchorage in 1915, where he started out as a photog-rapher in the old Carrol Building on Fourth Avenue. He later opened a studio in the Anchorage Hotel.

The young artist had traveled, studied and lived in Europe before heading north. Sources indicate he photographed events during the Boer War in South Africa and then worked as an artist for a British publication covering the Boxer Rebellion in China. Several of his paintings were accepted by the Royal Academy of Arts in London.

After coming to Alaska, his budding career took him south to Los Angeles and Seattle for a while. But he returned in 1934 and stayed at the Anchorage Hotel for the rest of his life. His studio was in the hotel lobby, and he lived upstairs.

"This is my last day on earth," Laurence, 75, told his second wife, Jeanne, on Sept. 12, 1940. He laid aside his paintbrush and started winding up his business affairs.

When Jeanne protested that he was just tired, he replied that he felt life slowly oozing out of his body. He then called the hospital and asked for a private room.

"The hotel doesn't like stiffs hanging around," he said.

Laurence's premonition was correct. He died that night. His nurse said she had never seen anyone leave this earth with such grace and dignity. As he lived, so he died.

1943: Venetie Reservation Created

In 1943, U.S. Secretary of the Interior Harold L. Ickes created the Venetie Reservation.

Venetie, pictured here in 1939, is located on the north side of the Chandalar River about 45 miles northwest of Fort Yukon. A man named Old Robert settled there in 1895 because fish and game were plentiful.

The U.S. Geological Survey in 1899 found around 50 Natives living near the area, known to early explorers as Old Robert's Village or Chandalar Village. But the gold rush to the Chandalar region in 1906 and 1907 brought many miners. They built about 40 cabins at Caro upriver from Venetie and a store near the mouth of the East Fork.

By 1910, most of the gold had played out, and the miners moved on.

Through combined efforts of the remaining residents of Venetie, Arctic Village, Christian Village and Robert's Fish Camp, the Venetie Indian Reservation was established to protect the land for subsistence use.

A school started at Venetie around the same time, which encouraged additional families to settle in the village. Eventually an airstrip, post office and store were built.

During the 1950s and 1960s, the use of seasonal camps declined, but the invention of snowmachines enabled Venetie residents to renew use of areas that traditionally had been occupied seasonally.

When the Alaska Native Claims Settlement Act passed in 1971, Venetie and Arctic Village opted for title to the 1.8 million acres of land in the former reservation, which they own as tenants in common through the Native Village of Venetie Tribal Government.

Jean Fredson teaches son Billy about beading in their Venetie home.

1944: Alaska-Juneau Gold Mine Shuts Down

Although the federal War Production Board ordered the closure of all nonessential mines to free up men for the World War II effort in 1942, it allowed the Alaska-Juneau Gold Mine to continue its operation.

But the operating costs proved too high to continue mining at rock-bottom prices, so the massive mine closed in 1944.

In its heyday, the A-J Mine produced millions of ounces of gold from the

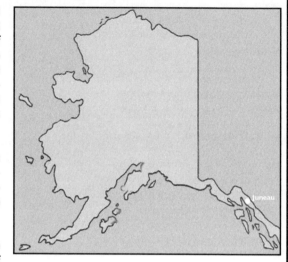

ore-bearing geological formation called the Juneau Gold Belt that stretches about 90 miles across the heart of the Alaska Panhandle.

The Juneau Gold Belt was one of the world's richest deposits of the precious metal, mining more than 8.8 million ounces up to 2006, and it was the earliest large-scale mining development in Alaska.

Prospectors first discovered gold at Juneau around 1880, which led to Juneau becoming a booming mining town 16 years before stampeders' pans filled with nuggets in the Klondike.

Three massive mills were created: the Alaska-Juneau at the southern end of Juneau, the Alaska-Gastineau farther south at Thane, and the Treadwell Gold Mining Co. across the Gastineau Channel on Douglas Island.

Treadwell's production peaked in 1915, and then it folded following a cave-in in 1917 that flooded three of its four mines. The Alaska-Gastineau shut down in 1921.

Juneau, which became Alaska's capital in 1906, turned toward tourism and commercial fishing to bolster its economy. And today, one out of every two workers are employed by the federal, state or local government.

Filipino "pickers" remove debris from an ore conveyer belt at the Alaska-Juneau Gold Mine in 1939.

1945: Floating Clinics Take to Alaska Waters

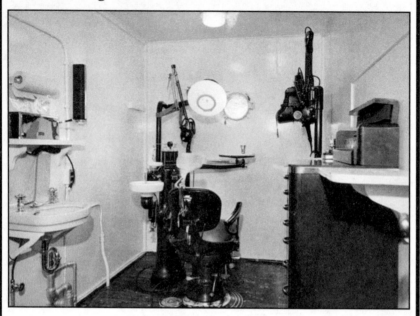

In post-World War II Alaska, the battle against tuberculosis was the territory's major health issue, especially among Alaska Natives. The crisis led to the creation of a unique health program overseen by Dr. C. Earl Albrecht, Alaska's first full-time Commissioner of Health.

Since most rural patients could not come to the cities for treatment, the treatment came to them in the form of mobile health units traveling on the roads, railroad and waterways.

The *M/V Health* and *M/V Hygiene* served those from the Alaska Peninsula to the Aleutian Islands to Western Alaska, and the *Yukon Health* tended to those who lived along the Yukon River.

The ships traveled between coastal communities each spring and/or fall. The doctors radioed ahead to let villagers know when they expected to be in port. The local people then would board for checkups and medical care, including teeth-pulling, shots and X-rays.

1947: Kake Becomes First Incorporated School District

Kake, located 95 air miles southwest of Juneau in Southeast Alaska, became the Territory of Alaska's first independently incorporated school district serving all Native children in 1947. Four years later, the U.S. Congress extended the provisions of the Johnson-O'Malley Act passed in 1934 to Alaska. The act provided a means of transferring the education of Native children from the federal government to state and local school systems.

The photograph above shows the Kake school in the early 1930s when it was a U.S. public school.

1947: Southeast Natives File Land Claims Suit

In 1947, Tlingit and Haida people filed the first land claims suit in the U.S. Court of Claims. Southeast Alaska Natives, like those pictured at this fish camp, wanted to get back their land and ensure subsistence use for future generations.

1947: Tongass Timber Act Passes Congress

The U. S. Congress passed the Tongass Timber Act in 1947. This law allowed the Secretary of Agriculture to enter into timber sale contracts, with the receipts to be deposited in a special fund until Native land claims in Southeast Alaska were resolved.

1947: Alaska Command Established

The U.S. military established the Alaska Command in 1947. It was the first unified command of the U.S. Army, Air Force and Navy.

In this photograph, maintenance support for Alaska Air Command's combat and mission support aircraft is provided by the 5040th Consolidated Aircraft Maintenance Group based at Elmendorf Air Force Base in Anchorage.

1948: ALCAN Opens to Civilian Traffic

The pioneer Alaska-Canada Highway was opened to civilians in late 1948, although there were some rough spots, as seen by this car plowing through mud near Lesser Slave Lake, Alberta, Canada.

COLD WAR ERA

20

'RED SCARE' BRINGS BOOM

A "Red Scare" gripped the nation following World War II. The Union of Soviet Socialist Republics, an ally during the war, became an international rival armed with nuclear power after it exploded its first atomic bomb and built an intercontinental bomber in late 1949.

And Alaska, offering the shortest route for a Soviet attack on America, became the "eyes" of the nation.

Schoolchildren were taught to "duck and cover" during the 1950s as a means of protecting themselves if a nuclear attack occurred. Immediately after they saw a flash, they were to stop what they were doing and get on the ground under cover — such as a table, or next to a wall — and assume the fetal position, lying facedown and covering their heads with their hands.

Congress quickly appropriated money to build up Alaskan Air Command facilities, which included an Aircraft Control and Warning system in the Last Frontier. The warning system consisted of 10 permanent radar facilities – five coastal surveillance sites, three Interior ground control and intercept sites, and two control centers.

Ladd Air Force Base in Fairbanks grew, and the Eielson Air Force Base, constructed in 1947 just 26 miles south of Alaska's Interior city, became more important. The military also expanded Elmendorf Air Force Base near Anchorage, U.S. Army bases at Fort Richardson and Big Delta, and U.S. Navy bases at Kodiak and Adak.

Following the June 1950 attack by communist-backed North Korea on democratic South Korea, the new air defense system went on around-the-clock watch. Many people thought that attack was just the beginning of Soviet leader Joseph Stalin's plan to take over the world.

Two workers climb the dome atop a White Alice facility at Cape Chiniak on Kodiak Island. The site was never activated because advances in technology allowed the Middleton Island site to provide better coverage for the area. Completed in the fall of 1957, it did provide Kodiak Island with long-distance telephone service until satellites took over in the 1970s.

COLD WAR ERA

Top left: Steamrollers compact ground being prepared for an airstrip 26 miles south of Ladd Air Field near Fairbanks in 1947.

Known as "26-Mile Strip," it originally served during World War II as an alternative landing area for planes ferried from Montana during the Russian lend-lease program. How it evolved into a U.S. Air Force base a few years later was determined by Mother Nature.

During the Cold War era, the military saw a need for a large bomber base. Initially, it chose property 29 miles south of Nenana and laid out a 14,500-foot runway, according to Air Force records. But while building temporary warehouses and wells, a series of earthquakes caused the military to reconsider the location. A fault ran across the center of the proposed runway.

Ladd Air Field in Fairbanks would not do either, since its 9,200-foot runway couldn't be expanded any more thanks to bends in the Chena River.

So the funds remaining from the aborted Nenana project were diverted to 26-Mile Strip and the existing runway was extended to 14,500 feet.

In 1948, Mile 26 Strip became Eielson Air Force Base.

That same year, the military began awarding contracts for building an early warning radar system throughout the territory. Since it had already withdrawn 16,000 acres near Nenana, it decided to construct Clear Air Force Station there.

Its history as a radar site jump-started in 1957 when the Soviet Union launched its satellite, Sputnik. Two years later, a 10- by 40-mile strip of wilderness at Clear was appropriated to become Site II of the Ballistic Missile Early Warning System.

Over the next two years, construction continued on three massive detection radars that became Clear's trademark. The radars, designed by GE and MIT's Lincoln Lab and built by RCA, measure 165 by 400 feet and weigh 2 million pounds apiece. Considering there were no major roads in the area at the time, the construction of Clear was an enormous undertaking with a final price tag of $360 million.

Bottom left: This aerial view of an Alaskan Air Command radar installation at Clear shows three AN/FPS-50 fixed detection radars. Clear was the second operational site in the billion-dollar system designed to provide early warning to the North American Air Defense Command should a missile attack be launched against the North American Continent.

Alaska's bush pilots helped deliver equipment that built the Distant Early Warning System in the 1950s. Pictured above is Sigurd Wien landing a Noorduyn Norseman six- to eight-seat airplane loaded with radar equipment at Cross Island, 20 miles off the Arctic coastline, about 250 miles east of Barrow. The man standing in the foreground is unidentified.

By the mid-1950s, more defense money poured into the territory to build an infrastructure capable of keeping the Russians at bay. The federal government spent more than $1 billion on an ultra-modern radar network, called the Distant Early Warning System, with sites located near the Arctic Circle. When completed in early 1957, it had 57 sites spaced 100 miles apart and stretched from the northwestern tip of Alaska to Cape Dyer in eastern Canada. It also expanded down the Aleutian Chain.

Soon Alaska's sparse communities became connected in a way that never could have happened without military money.

Radio and telephone support systems for the DEW line popped up on the tundra, as Alaska Integrated Communications Enterprise linked communications between the DEW line and aircraft warning networks. Most Alaskans came to know these integrated points as White Alice sites after the military added "White" to its code name in front of the acronym.

Thirty-four White Alice sites relayed information to military personnel at the Elmendorf and Eielson Air Force bases. These sites

Alaskan Air Command fighters were stationed at bases in King Salmon and Galena, pictured above, to keep watch over Russians entering U.S. airspace.

offered jobs in small villages and helped develop cash economies where subsistence lifestyles had been the rule of thumb. They also brought television, radio and telephone communications – as well as interracial marriages – that introduced new cultures to Native communities.

Bases at Galena and King Salmon were reactivated, too. Originally built during World War II as rest and refueling stops for the lend-lease program, which ferried American planes to the Soviet Union for use on the Russian front when we were allies, these bases became instrumental in intercepting Russian aircraft foraying into U.S. airspace during the Cold War. At the height of the Soviet bomber threat in the mid-1950s, six Alaskan Air Command fighter-interceptor squadrons were based in Alaska.

Following the Soviet-backed coup in Czechoslovakia and the blockade of Berlin in 1948 and 1949, the U.S. Air Force deployed Lockheed F-80 aircraft, called Shooting Stars, at the reactivated King Salmon base.

Hundreds of miles of 70-pound rails and wooden bridges, like those pictured here, were replaced by 115-pound rails and new steel bridges along the Alaska Railroad route.

While defense dollars bolstered the military presence in Alaska, money rolled into the territory to overhaul the Alaska Railroad, too. An old roundhouse in Fairbanks was transformed into a $7.5 million terminal; Anchorage received a diesel-mechanical building, power plant and employee housing; steel bridges replaced wooden ones along the route, and hundreds of miles of 115-pound rails were laid where 70-pound ones had worn out between Anchorage and Fairbanks and Anchorage and Seward. Daily passenger service between Anchorage and Fairbanks began on June 18, 1951.

The road system in the Last Frontier benefited, as well. Between 1945 and 1952, the Glenn Highway was improved and blacktopped, the Richardson Highway was rebuilt and hard-surfaced, the road between Seward and Anchorage was built, the Alaska-Canada Highway opened to civilian traffic and the Sterling Highway connected Homer to the road system.

During the 1950s, Alaska became important as a transportation hub for personnel, equipment and supplies as America became more involved in other conflicts around the world, including Vietnam.

And while several Alaska communities benefited from billions in military spending during this Cold War era, Anchorage in Southcentral

The influx of military during the Cold War era boosted Anchorage's population dramatically between 1950 and 1960.

Alaska reaped most of the benefits as more military personnel arrived in town and made it home. By 1952, it was the fastest-growing city in North America, on the basis of percentage rate of growth, according to Clarence C. Hulley, author of "Alaska Past and Present."

21

ANCHORAGE: JEWEL ON THE TUNDRA

B y the early 1950s, the tent city at the mouth of Ship Creek had turned into a bustling, modern city thanks to federal money pouring in for military defense. Servicemen and women who had been stationed in Alaska chose to remain after World War II, and additional military projects during the Cold War era brought thousands more construction workers north.

Anchorage had yet to see its first traffic light when this photo of Fourth Avenue and H Street was taken in 1947. Businesses shown include Piggly Wiggly grocery, The Club, O.K. Cleaners, First National Bank, Merchant's Cafe, South Seas Nite Club and Carol's Dress Shop.

During the 1920s and 1930s, Anchorage Light and Power Co. built a dam at Eklutna Lake, seen here.

But the town, which in 1947 didn't have one traffic light, found itself playing catch-up to a demand for services and goods as frame houses, trailers and tar paper shacks sprouted up in subdivisions like Mountain View, Eastchester, Rogers Park and Spenard.

Reliable power for the growing populace soon became a major problem. Blackouts became frequent, prices were high and many homes had no electricity at all.

Anchorage Light and Power Co. stepped up power production in 1947. The company, which had tamed Eklutna Creek and built a hydroelectric plant – about 30 miles northeast of Anchorage – during the 1920s and 1930s, leased and then bought the stern half of a wrecked ocean-going tanker named *Sakett's Harbor*. The hulk was beached at the mouth of Ship Creek, and by using the wreck's boilers and generating equipment, the power company was able to provide almost half the electricity needed by the ever-growing Anchorage area. But the power situation became critical the next year.

The Bureau of Reclamation found a solution to Anchorage's power problem in 1948.

"The use of electric power in the power market area is expanding so rapidly that new installations of hydroelectric power plants are needed as quickly as possible to meet the emergency requirements

Two construction workers stand at the entrance to the Eklutna power plant water tunnel. A railway line and large diameter pipe are visible going into the tunnel. The Eklutna dam, power plant and tunnel – called the Eklutna Project – were constructed between 1951 and 1955 by the Bureau of Reclamation and cost more than $33 million.

of existing loads and to permit the establishment of new industries to support increases in population and economic development," said Joseph Morgan, chief of the Alaska Investigations Office, in a 1948 report to the Commissioner of Reclamation.

The project, authorized on July 31, 1950, included a new dam to raise the level of Eklutna Lake to 875 feet above sea level with an intake tunnel at 830 feet.

During the four-year construction period, successful bidder Palmer Constructors paid about 155 workers a wage of $2.74 per hour. Crane operators made a high of $3.57 per hour, and divers received $40 per six-hour shift, according to government records.

That project, completed in 1955 at a cost of more than $33 million, and the formation of another power company, Chugach Electric Cooperative, ensured a secure future with plenty of power for the people of Anchorage.

Breakfast	
Ham & Eggs, including	
Toast, potatoes and coffee	$ 1.50
Small tomato juice	.35
Large tomato juice	.50
Large orange juice	.75
Lunch	
Sandwiches	$ .50 and up
Deluxe hamburger	$ 1.15
Dinner	
Fish	$ 1.75
Roast beef	$ 2.20
T-bone steak	$ 4.00
Salads	
Fruit	$ 2.25
Crab	2.50
Lettuce	2.15
Cole slaw	.65
Donuts	$ .35
Coffee	.15

A typical menu in 1950s Anchorage looked something like this, according to a diary entry made by Phyllis Downing Carlson in 1955.

Above: Pressures of the Cold War between the United States and the Soviet Union ensured continued heavy military investment in the Anchorage area after World War II, as seen in this photograph of new barracks at Elmendorf Air Force Base in 1947.

Below: KENI went on the air in 1948. Owned by millionaire industrialist Austin E. "Cap" Lathrop, the radio station was housed in a two-story art deco building built of concrete. Other businesses seen in this 1950s view of downtown Anchorage include Woolworth's, SAS, 4th Avenue Theatre, First National Bank of Anchorage and the Reed Building.

Above: Alaska Airlines, Cheechako Tavern, Hewitt's Drug Store and Anchorage Appliance are seen from the northeast corner of Fourth Avenue and E Street in 1949 Anchorage.

Below: Sled dogs parked along Anchorage streets were commonplace during the 1940s and 1950s.

The Old Federal Building on Fourth Avenue between F and G streets brought pride and respectability to the little town built along Ship Creek when erected in 1939. It was the first permanent federal government building in Anchorage.

But its construction might not have happened without a little trickery.

It all began when the townspeople learned that U.S. Postmaster General James A. Farley was slated to visit Anchorage in 1936. To highlight the woefully inadequate post office, built in 1915, some local leaders banded together to highlight its shortcomings – and to add a few touches of their own.

They lugged all the good furniture out of the building and replaced it with broken tables, cracked chairs and other pieces that had seen better days. Buckets placed on the floor in strategic spots left no doubt that the deteriorating roof had a serious leaking problem. And signs announcing "Unsafe," "Condemned," "Dangerous" and "Watch Out For Falling Debris" were nailed up for good measure.

The plan worked. Anchorage officials even convinced Postmaster Farley to turn over the first spade full of dirt at a site where they thought the new government building should go up.

It took the U.S. Congress two years to approve its construction and appropriate $1 million toward the cause. The official name carved on the building was United States Post Office and Court House, but it was known as the Federal Building.

The Sisters of Providence built this two-story, 52-bed hospital at Ninth Avenue and L Street in 1939, and it served Anchorage's medical needs until the early 1960s.

A great building boom brought modern steel and concrete structures, office buildings, hotels, hospitals and apartment buildings to the community. By 1950, it also boasted automatic telephone service, parking meters, traffic lights, home mail delivery and a symphony orchestra comprised of 17 volunteers. Anchorage was well on its way to becoming the largest and most modern city in the territory.

Clifford Cernick wrote that it was much like Baghdad in an article appearing in the Seattle Times on March 4, 1951 – a time when Baghdad was a bustling city, a jewel in the desert.

"A grizzled prospector, back in Anchorage after three years in the Alaska wilderness, noted the towering framework of a new apartment building, the paved streets, the bustling downtown traffic and glistening shops.

"Nudging his companion, he declared: 'Hey! Look what they've gone and done to Anchorage!'"

Above: A high-rise apartment building was built at 1200 L Street during the 1950s.

Below: This view from the ninth floor of the L Street Apartments is looking toward downtown Anchorage in the mid-1950s.

COLD WAR ERA

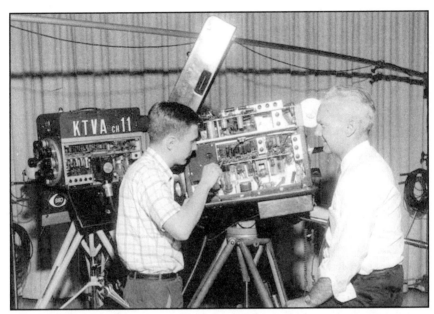

Above: KTVA, Anchorage's first television station, began broadcasting in 1953 with veteran broadcaster August G. "Augie" Hiebert, right, at the helm.

Below: This mid-1950s aerial view shows midtown, center, and downtown Anchorage at the right. Mount Susitna and Cook Inlet are in the background.

Cernick wrote that old-time prospectors, Natives from remote Bering Sea villages and most tourists from the states all thought Anchorage was an amazing town.

"Mingled with the town's frontier atmosphere is a new spirit of feverish construction and growth. It is a city reaching for the clouds, with one 14-story building planned and several others on the drawing boards," Cernick wrote.

"The average statesider's conception of life in the 'ice-locked land of glaciers, totem poles and Eskimos' is shattered forever when he notes the city's modern buildings, its three radio stations, three theaters, two newspapers and well-stocked shops."

He added that the downtown area was a hub of activity.

"Along Fourth and Fifth avenues – the city's main stems – frontier-type honky-tonks stand side by side with gay, sophisticated night

This late 1950s aerial view of downtown Anchorage, with the Park Strip in the center and Alaska Railroad running along the bottom, shows a growing city.

Alyeska Resort, seen here, was built south of Anchorage in Girdwood in 1954.

clubs. Multicolored neons splash glittering pools of color across the wide, paved streets at night."

Cernick noted that women in fashionable mink coats were as much a part of the Anchorage landscape as Native women wearing moose-hide parkas. And that dogs and sleds didn't warrant any more notice than panel delivery trucks. He said it was normal to see business executives and bank presidents sharing lunch counters with trappers and prospectors.

The reporter said the contrast and modern style of the town caused one airline pilot to make the observation that struck Cernick as fitting.

"An airline pilot, arriving over Anchorage at night after the long flight from Tokyo and seeing for the first time its pattern of flickering lights, winking like jewels in the midst of a vast, forbidding wilderness, described the city as a 'Tundra Baghdad.' In many respects, the name fits.

Anchorage built a canal to connect Lake Spenard to Lake Hood in 1940. Seen above near the new airport in 1959, it made the waterway the world's largest seaplane base.

By the 1950s, Anchorage had became known as the "air crossroad of the world," with stops by air carriers from the Orient to the continental United States.

"Since the Second World War, the city has been charging ahead like a downriver steamer at full speed," Cernick wrote. "In 1940, the census credited Anchorage with a population of 3,495. Today, the city proper has 11,060, and when suburban areas are counted, the total is close to 30,000.

"In the past few years, a city-wide swath of cleared land has been moving steadily southward. Hundreds of settlers have come and have constructed homes, roads and streets. ..."

The area east of Anchorage was filling with many newcomers, too. On May 13, 1949, 850 people put their names in a hat for the right to homestead. The list of names of those drawn to homestead 160 acres reads like a current East Anchorage street map – Dick Turpin, Burl Tudor, Von Baxter, Paul Boniface and Arnold Muldoon.

By 1952, the town on the tundra had more than 40,000 residents, according to Clarence C. Hulley, author of "Alaska Past and Present."

Anchorage earned the honor of becoming the first All-America City outside of the contiguous 48 states in 1956. Businesses in this view of Fourth Avenue include Hewitt's Drug Store, Anchorage Radio & Television, Cheechako Tavern & Cafe, Alaska Airlines, Carlquist Jewelers, Yukon Stationers, Shimeks, Koslosky's Store for Men, D & D Bar & Café and Denali Theatre. The McKinley Building sits in the background.

But when the outlying 10-mile radius was considered, that number jumped to 100,000 – 25,000 of which were military personnel.

Not all Alaskans were pleased with Anchorage's cosmopolitan evolution.

"An Alaskan old-timer named 'Russian Jack' is not too happy about what he calls 'all this hustle and bustle.' Gazing down traffic-choked Fourth Avenue, the city's main thoroughfare, Jack remembers he 'used to hunt moose there,'" Cernick wrote.

However, noted Cernick, the "city's younger generation, unhampered by memories of the past, is looking to the promise-filled future – the not-too-distant time when Anchorage will rival many of the large cities in the States."

The National Municipal League and Look magazine named Anchorage an "All-America City" in 1956 for "successfully tackling a skyrocketing population that threatened to swamp city facilities and pushing for needed civic improvements." It was the first time that any city outside of the contiguous 48 states had been so honored.

The influx of people following World War II, along with improvements to the road system, gave Matanuska Valley farmers a market for their fresh produce – some of which found its way into this Piggly Wiggly grocery store in Anchorage during the 1950s.

22

OTHER ALASKA TOWNS GROW

A nchorage wasn't the only city to benefit from defense spending during the Cold War era. But other towns only received modest population increases and monetary benefits during the 1950s.

Fairbanks

Expansion of Ladd Air Field and construction of Eielson Air Force Base brought more military personnel to Fairbanks, seen here in the 1950s.

A military truck drives down the north side of Second Street from Cushman Street, looking east toward Lacy Street. The businesses, from the left, are a gift shop, Griffin's Music (and photography), the Model Café, the Pantorium Cleaners, Alaska Airlines, The Daily-News Miner, Lomen's Equipment, Sky Lounge and Cottage Bar, and Lathrop Enterprises (including a hotel, radio station and the Lacey Street Theater).

Fairbanks saw a post-war boom through the construction of Eielson Air Force Base and the enlargement of Ladd Air Force Base. Those projects brought more military personnel to Alaska's largest Interior city, which meant work for local residents and sales for city merchants.

The incorporated city's population in 1950 was pegged at 5,771 – an increase of about 2,200 from 1940, according to U.S. Census records. But its military population grew from 10 to more than 25,000 in the same time frame.

And unlike Anchorage, which had been carefully laid out by engineers back in 1915, the gold-rush town of Fairbanks just grew as defense money flowed in. Log cabins and makeshift shacks stood next to modern buildings like the Northward and Polaris.

Sources say that Fairbanks was owned by two families during the 1950s: the Lavery's, who owned Lavery's Grocery Store on Cushman Street, as well as most of the southern side of town, and the Lathrop family, who owned the north side of town. The influx of military personnel was a boon for them and other store owners.

Not all Fairbanks' businesses flourished during the Cold War era.

Following World War II, the Alaska-Canada Highway opened to civilian traffic, which meant delivery trucks could haul items to Alaska and bring competition to local stores. Soon products began arriving via the road system, as well as by air.

One business couldn't compete in the new marketplace. Creamer's Dairy, pictured above in 1950, had to close its doors.

Creamer's history goes back to 1904 when Charles and Belle Hinckley opened for business on Fourth Avenue. The Hinckley dairy moved to several acres across the Chena River in 1915 and served the community until it was sold to Charles and Anna Creamer in 1928.

The Creamers modernized the dairy and expanded business during the 1930s and 1940s. They built two large barns and sold milk, ice cream, cottage cheese and other dairy products throughout World War II.

But the Alaska-Canada Highway and increased airline traffic allowed competitors into the market, and by the late 1950s the dairy was struggling. It stopped production in 1966.

The state acquired the land in the early 1970s and turned it into a waterfowl sanctuary. The buildings, which still stand, are on the National Register of Historic Places.

Nome

The gold-rush era town of Nome, seen here in 1957, once boasted more than 20,000 people. But after the gold-laden sands had panned out, its population dropped to a steady 2,000. As the chief distributing center for Northwestern Alaska, military activity spurred construction of a new hospital, seawall and a few new hotels.

Seward

As the ocean terminal for the Alaska Railroad, Seward's population grew during and after World War II. The Seward Highway, completed in 1951, finally connected Seward to Anchorage and Alaska's growing road system. The community's population more than doubled from 900 people in 1940 to 2,100 by 1950.

Cordova

Above: Cordova, located near the mouth of the Copper River on the east side of Prince William Sound, once relied on the Kennecott copper mines for its income. When the mines shut down in 1938, the community turned to the fishing industry to keep it afloat. The town, which had about 1,200 residents in 1950, also became known as the razor clam capital of the world.

Below: To promote the razor clam industry, the Warrenton Clam Co. created this advertisement of two men digging a larger-than-life razorback clam.

Valdez

Valdez, which served as the gateway to the gold of the Tanana region at the turn-of-the-last century, declined after the Alaska Railroad chose Seward as its terminus in 1915. The building and improvements made to the Richardson Highway during the postwar years brought new life to the fishing community. By 1950, about 600 people lived in the Prince William Sound town, seen here.

Kodiak

Kodiak, home of a chief naval base in Alaska, received millions in government spending between 1950 and 1960 for a satellite tracking system. Military personnel comprised most of the 8,000 people in the district – the town itself only had about 2,000 residents.

Juneau

Alaska's territorial capital, built on the side of Mount Roberts in Southeast Alaska, didn't benefit much from the Cold War-era infusion of money. Its population remained relatively stable at 8,000, and most salaries were paid by the local, territorial and federal government. Businesses in this 1950 photograph looking east along Front Street from Seward Street include Juneau Drug Co., Gross Theater and Percy's Café.

Ketchikan

During the 1930s, Ketchikan – the center of Alaska's salmon industry – was Alaska's largest city.

Like Juneau, the Southeast community is built on the side of a mountain and its population hovered around 8,000 throughout the war and subsequent Cold War era.

Petersburg

Petersburg, known as the shrimp capital of Alaska, relied on the fishing industry for its livelihood during the war and postwar years. Located on the north end of the Wrangell Narrows, between Ketchikan and Juneau, this southeastern community had about 1,200 people in 1952.

Sitka

One of the oldest towns in Alaska, Sitka reaped a renewal during the war and postwar years. The U.S. military built a naval base on Japonski Island, and the federal government spent millions on hospitals, schools and other institutions in the coastal town of 3,000.

Skagway

Skagway, 90 miles northwest of Juneau, sprang to life during World War II. Once a booming supply center for stampeders heading to the Klondike gold fields at the turn-of-the-last century, the little coastal town dwindled to about 600 people before hostilities erupted in the 1940s. But as the terminus for the White Pass & Yukon Railway, its deserted streets filled with nearly 3,000 military men who guarded the coast and built the Alaska-Canada Highway. Its population dropped dramatically to pre-World War II numbers by the 1950s.

Wrangell

Wrangell saw a slow, steady increase during World War II and the Cold War era, but not due to defense dollars. This Southeastern town of about 1,500 people cultivated tourism for a source of income, as well as developed a sawmill, a marble quarry and its salmon industry.

23

Tuberculosis: The Alaska Scourge

A s defense funds to fight communism flowed into Alaska during the Cold War, Alaska's Natives were battling another enemy. Tuberculosis. Called the Alaska Scourge, it ravaged villages across the territory during the 1940s and 1950s.

"No population group in the world had as much TB as rural Alaska," said Dr. Robert Fraser, chief of the communicable disease

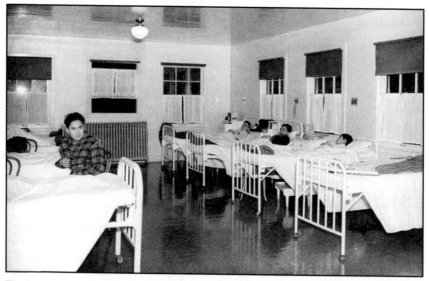

These young Native boys are trying to beat tuberculosis at the Bureau of Indian Affairs hospital in Juneau.

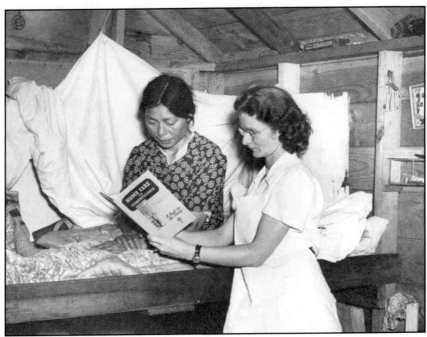
A nurse and patient in Nome review a manual titled "Home care of tuberculosis. A guide for the family," published in 1943.

section of the Alaska Department of Health and Social Services in an article by Wallace Turner published in the New York Times on July 3, 1983.

The disease persisted in the remote villages partly because medical care was sparse and partly because the conditions under which Native Alaskans lived was conducive to its spread. TB is transmitted mainly through droplets exhaled into the air when a victim coughs or spits. From first contact with a carrier, it didn't take long for others to start experiencing a persistent cough, night sweats, weight loss and chest pains.

Segregation of active TB cases was not easy among Alaska Natives because families were large and lived together in small spaces – often sleeping in the same bed, according to an article titled "A General View of Tuberculosis in Alaska" written by A. Holmes Johnson for the medical journal Chest.

Christine Kosbruk died of tuberculosis soon after marrying. Her father holds her casket.

"These Native people are a happy lot – one might say, 'happy-go-lucky.' They have a great sense of humor. When they are in health nothing can worry them. Consequently, no matter how serious an aspect the doctor puts on the condition, the tuberculosis patient, as soon as he has recovered from his more distressing symptoms and is beginning to feel better, regardless of multiple warnings, unvaryingly gets up and about, goes to the dances in which he so much delights – and returns to bed with an extension of the infection."

And the infected person, who felt good enough to enjoy the company of his fellow villagers, passed the disease along to others in no time at all.

There were no funds for a territorial sanitarium in 1940 when the disease began to flourish. The Territorial Department of Public Welfare had just enough funds for 40 cases to be sent south, so a few who were diagnosed went to hospitals in Seattle. Another 60 beds in Bureau of Indian Affairs hospitals also were available for TB patients.

Cases of tuberculosis began rising rapidly during World War II. Of 1,322 deaths reported in the territory in 1943, in Natives 21 percent were from TB compared to 1 percent of all deaths in non-Natives.

Alaska's first sanatorium opened about three miles out of Skagway right after the war. The hospital was actually an abandoned U.S. Army complex, and nurses described conditions for the 90 patients as drafty.

"Snow filtered through the plywood walls," nurse Betty Sorrels later recalled in a biographical sketch for the Juneau-Douglas City Museum. "The medical staff used canvas as bedspreads to aid in keeping the patients warm. The few windows were covered with a constant sheet of frost and ice."

The territory opened a 150-bed sanatorium in Seward during 1946, under the auspices of the Wesleyan Ladies Auxiliary, in buildings erected at the U.S. Army's decommissioned Fort Raymond. Called the "San," it could accommodate more than 100 patients and was a major employer in Seward after the war.

A U.S. Navy facility, including its boathouse, on Japonski Island near Sitka was renovated the following year. This 200-bed sanatorium

Tuberculosis patients sent to Sitka, shown here, could see Mount Edgecumbe in the background.

Above: The *M/V Hygiene* traveled to Alaska's coastal communities to see patients.

Below: The *M/V Health* visited Dutch Harbor and Unalaska to provide medical care.

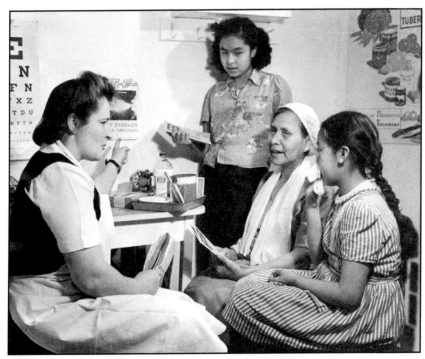

Above: A nurse talks to patients about tuberculosis on board the *M/V Hygiene*.

Alaska's first full-time commissioner of health, Dr. C. Earl Albrecht, responded to a health crisis brought on by tuberculosis across the territory by instituting "floating clinics" in 1945.

The *Yukon Health* tended to villagers' medical needs along the Yukon River. Coastal villagers – from the Alaska Peninsula to the Aleutian Islands to Western Alaska – were served by the *M/V Health* and *Hygiene*. Juneau was the home port for the "health boats," as well as headquarters for the Territorial Department of Health.

Motoring between the coastal communities each spring and/or fall, the ships would radio ahead to each village, letting the villagers know when they expected to anchor. At the ship's horn, local people would take their skiffs out for a checkup or on-the-spot medical care.

Children nicknamed these vessels "shot ships," because the stops also meant vaccinations against smallpox, measles and other diseases.

Tuberculosis gripped schoolchildren like these in Barrow. Only six of 30 first-graders lived to finish the 1947 school year.

was for children with bone tuberculosis, and patients from Skagway were moved there in February 1947.

A schoolteacher in Barrow reported that of 30 children ages 5 to 6 who entered school at the beginning of the 1946-1947 school year, only six lived to finish. Another survey showed that three-quarters of the children in the Yukon-Kuskokwim Delta had the disease.

As cases of tuberculosis mounted, Alaska leaders became more alarmed and a few traveled to Washington, D.C., to bring the territory's health crisis to the attention of the U.S. Congress.

While testifying before a Congressional hearing in 1948, Alaska Territorial Gov. Ernest Gruening told the legislators that the TB death rate for Alaska Natives was around 16 times the national average.

Thanks to the eye-opening information provided by Gruening, territorial Sen. Edward Lewis "Bob" Bartlett and Dr. C. Earl Albrecht, the territory's first official Commissioner of Health, Congress appropriated more than $1 million to help Alaska fight the disease in 1949.

The Alaska Grant money was used to set up control programs, establish a TB register, administer vaccines and deliver health services. Another grant was used to build a TB facility at Mount Edgecumbe near Sitka, a 400-bed hospital in Anchorage and 25-bed hospitals at Barrow, Kotzebue, Bethel and Kanakanak, near Dillingham.

Some Alaska Natives, many leaving home for the first time, spent months – sometimes years – trying to regain their health at medical facilities like the Alaska Native Service Hospital in Anchorage, seen above in the mid-1950s, or Mount Edgecumbe Medical Center, seen below in 1951.

The Parran report of 1954 detailed the territory's health program, especially the issue of tuberculosis. Pictured at the table are, from left, Dr. Antonio Ciocco, Dr. Thomas Parran, Dr. C. Earl Albrecht, Dr. James A. Crabtree and Dr. Walter J. McNerney.

For many Alaska Natives, going to one of these treatment centers was their first long stay away from their villages. Treatment often lasted years, and the patients had a tough time being away from family, friends and familiar surroundings. Also, many patients didn't speak English, which added to the frightening experience.

A study led by Dr. Thomas Parran, former surgeon general of the U.S. Public Health Service, conducted on Alaska Native health during 1953-54 yielded shocking results and led to reformation in the health system.

"... 'Native Alaska' ... and 'White Alaska' ... represent extremes in the health status of their citizens. White Alaska, with a relatively young, vigorous, generally urbanized population, shows a record of life expectancy as favorable as that in the majority of the states. Its problems are those of every new and growing country. ... In tragic contrast, the indigenous peoples of Native Alaska are the victims of sickness, crippling conditions and premature deaths to a degree exceeded in very few parts of the world. Among them, health problems are nearly out of hand. If other Americans could see for themselves the large numbers of tuberculosis, the crippled, the blind, the deaf, the malnourished, the desperately ill among a relatively small

These Boy Scouts helped put up posters urging people to get chest X-rays.

population, private generosity would dispatch shiploads of food and clothing for Alaska, alongside the cargoes setting out for Korea; doctors and nurses would be mobilized and equipped with the urgency of great hospital units in wartime; the Alaska missions would not need to beg for support."

After the U.S. Public Health Service assumed responsibility for all services previously overseen by the federal Bureau of Indian Affairs in 1955, it launched a determined attack against tuberculosis. With technological advances and medical progress during World War II, along with improved air transportation and more funding, the Public Health Service made great inroads to stomping out TB in Alaska's villages. Native populations surged in direct response to the TB control programs – as well as the creation of streptomycin, improvement in health care and nutrition.

The heroic fight against tuberculosis in Alaska continued into the 1980s and helped to dramatically drop the death rate for the disease. In 1946, tuberculosis was listed as the cause of death on 43 percent of all death certificates for Alaska Natives. From 1980-1989, only 13 of 19,820 Alaskans died from active tuberculosis, according to state Department of Health and Social Services records.

The federal Department of Health sent Mobile Health Units to help patients living along the territory's road system. Workers, like those pictured here, also traveled via the Alaska Railroad to reach people in need.

ROAD TO STATEHOOD

24

EARLY MOVERS & SHAKERS

After Alaska became a territory of the United States in 1912, its non-voting delegate to Congress began to battle for statehood. Judge James Wickersham, elected to serve the then-possession in 1908, pounded the halls of Congress trying to muster support.

Alaska had about 58,000 residents when Wickersham introduced the first statehood bill in 1916. The bill didn't go anywhere, however, because most members of Congress, as well as the American public, thought Alaska wasn't ready for admittance to the Union.

But the sparsely populated North Country was used to people missing the big picture when it came to the Last Frontier. After Alaska became a possession of the United States in 1867, the federal government basically ignored it for the first few decades.

Things began to change when prospectors in 1880 discovered rich veins of gold on Douglas Island, across from what became Juneau in Southeast Alaska. Hundreds of white miners headed north.

Those newcomers clamored for Congress to set up a civilian government so they could stake mining claims and get title to land. But they faced a monumental challenge, as public opinion was not on their side.

"The total white population of Alaska is about 250 and, for purposes of political illustration, the number of voters is usually put

Hundreds of miners streamed into Southeast Alaska following the discovery of gold on Douglas Island in 1880. Housing became a priority, as seen by this photograph of barracks built in Thane, about 4 miles southeast of Juneau.

down at 15 ... To give this handful of people a governor and a representative in Congress, to say nothing of the courts, would be a farce of the broadest kind," reported a New York Times editorial on March 22, 1880.

Undaunted, miners in Juneau held a convention in 1881 and elected a former Confederate officer, Mottrom Ball, as their unofficial delegate to the U.S. House of Representatives.

While Congress did not accept his credentials, it did allocate money for Ball's expenses as he lobbied to extend government to Alaska. Those efforts paid off a few years later.

Through the Organic Act of 1884, Congress provided Alaska with the bare essentials of government. It did not authorize a legislature, but it did make Sitka the temporary capital and allowed for a district court, a governor, a district attorney and a U.S. marshal.

U.S. President Chester A. Arthur appointed John H. Kinkead as Alaska's first governor in 1884.

The new appointee arrived with "an immense supply of cases labeled 'canned tomatoes.' These 'tomatoes' were proclaimed as tasting exactly like Scotch whiskey and producing the same effect," noted Presbyterian missionary S.H. Young, according to the Alaska History and Cultural Studies Web site.

Kinkead served for less than a year and was replaced by Alfred P. Swineford when Grover Cleveland became president.

John H. Kinkead, who was appointed Alaska's first governor in 1884, served less than a year.

More governors followed, always "outsiders," and according to political scientist Melvin Crain, they had little to do.

The first governors "had practically no civil duties to perform except to inspect, report and to enforce a handful of contradictory laws, with no enforcement means provided," according to Crain.

Following the Klondike Gold Rush near the turn-of-the-last century, Congress adopted a new civil code that allowed communities of 300 or more to incorporate with seven-member city councils and three-member school boards.

The civil code of 1900 also set up new judicial districts, specified what activities were illegal and assigned punishments for violations. In 1905, Congress moved Alaska's capital to Juneau, which had grown from the mining boom. It also made provisions for the civil government to obtain taxes through business licenses – that led to the age-old battle cry "no taxation without representation."

Congress began to listen to pleas from its northern-most possession to authorize a delegate for the District of Alaska.

"The universal opinion among all classes in Alaska is that the District should be represented by a delegate in Congress," reported a Senate subcommittee in 1903.

But Congress did not act.

Three years later, residents of Valdez took matters into their own hands. They sent newly elected President Theodore Roosevelt the following message on inauguration day 1906:

"On behalf of 60,000 American citizens who are denied the right of representation in any form, we demand, in mass meeting assembled, that Alaska be annexed to Canada."

That year, Congress finally allowed Alaskans to have one non-voting member in the U.S. House of Representatives.

Early delegates fought for the right to elect a legislature so Alaskans could have a representative government instead of being under the rule of dozens of federal agencies and appointees.

Wickersham, who came to Alaska in 1900 after being appointed as a district court judge by President William McKinley, became the most powerful and influential of those early delegates. During his tenure, he fought against big companies that wanted to dominate Alaska's resources and future – specifically J.P. Morgan and the Guggenheims, who were involved in copper mining in the Wrangell Mountains and shipping.

As Alaska's non-voting delegate from 1908 to 1920 and 1931 to 1932, James Wickersham persuaded Congress to pass legislation that greatly benefited Alaska. Among his accomplishments are winning home rule for Alaska as a territory in 1912, obtaining funds for construction of the Alaska Railroad in 1914, opening the Alaska Agricultural College and School of Mining in 1917 – which later became the University of Alaska – and introducing the first statehood bill in 1916, 43 years before it became a reality.

Ten years after his death on Oct. 23, 1939, the Alaska Territorial Legislature paid tribute to his memory by designating his birthday, Aug. 24, as Wickersham Day.

Alaska's first Territorial Senate, pictured here, met in March 1913 at Elks Hall in Juneau.

"The central political issue in Alaska, as Wickersham phrased it, was whether the territory would have government rule or Guggenheim rule," said University of Alaska Fairbanks historian Terrence Cole in an article for Alaska History and Cultural Studies.

Thanks to Wickersham's tireless efforts, Alaska became a territory with the passage of the Second Organic Act of 1912. Now Alaskans could seat an elected legislature.

When Wickersham passed the Congressional delegate torch to Anthony J. Dimond in 1932, companies outside the territory dominated the salmon industry, as well.

By the early 20th century, canned salmon was the largest industry in the territory and generated 80 percent of the territorial tax revenues, according to fisheries historian Bob King in "Sustaining Alaska's Fisheries: Fifty Years of Statehood." King documented the history of the industry for the Alaska Department of Fish and Game.

The industry used fish traps, which captured the majority of fish entering Alaska's waterways. At one time more than 800 fish traps were in operation, primarily in Southeast Alaska and Prince William Sound.

Anthony J. Dimond, born in New York, came north as a gold prospector in 1904 and started practicing law in Valdez in 1913. His political career blossomed in that Prince William Sound town. Dimond served as its mayor from 1920-1922 and 1925-1932. He also was elected to the Alaska Territorial Senate and then served as Alaska's non-voting delegate to Congress from 1932-1944.

When his secretary, E.L. "Bob" Bartlett, became the territory's delegate in 1944, Dimond accepted a position as district judge in Alaska's 3rd Judicial District.

Dimond died on May 28, 1953. Alaskans now celebrate Nov. 30 as Anthony Dimond Day, and in Anchorage, A.J. Dimond High School and Dimond Boulevard are named after him.

Alaskans were united in their hatred of fish traps, like the one shown here. They caught most fish heading to spawn in the waterways.

Alaskans hated the use of these traps, which decimated fish populations and local fishermen's livelihoods. Alaskan workers and communities didn't see the profits from this highly efficient fishery, either. The salmon packing companies brought in workers from the Lower 48 and didn't pay them until they returned south.

By the mid-1940s, most Alaskans were fed up with federal agencies and outside companies controlling their destiny. They didn't like the fact that natural resources, especially mining and fishing, were controlled by interests in the Lower 48 – with profits flowing out of Alaska.

As citizens of a territory, they had no official voice in Washington, D.C., and they couldn't change the status quo. By a vote of 3-2, a special election in 1946 showed that most of the territory's residents approved of Alaska becoming a state.

Following that majority vote, the job of getting Congress on board with the idea fell on the shoulders of Edward Lewis "Bob" Bartlett.

Bartlett, who followed Dimond as Alaska's non-voting delegate in 1944, knew the ropes in Washington, D.C. He'd served as Dimond's secretary there during the 1930s.

He worked hard for statehood in the 1940s. But the powerful salmon packing companies, along with mining and shipping interests, lobbied harder to keep Alaska a territory. If it became a state, they would face more oversight, higher taxes and reduced profits.

Many people also questioned whether Alaska, with its small population, could support itself as a member of the Union. However, the influx of military into the territory following World War II dramatically changed the way America looked at the Last Frontier and gave statehood proponents hope for the future.

25

STATEHOOD MOMENTUM BUILDS

T he 1950s blew winds of change into the Last Frontier. World War II and the Cold War era brought billions of dollars north, which funded construction of military bases, roads, airfields and more. Thousands of retired and active troops also chose to make Alaska home.

Following World War II and the Cold War era, many active and retired military people stayed in Alaska. This group is posing in front of the Eielson Memorial Building on the campus of the Alaska Agricultural College and School of Mining in Fairbanks. The building was dedicated to Alaska aviator Carl "Ben" Eielson.

The newcomers were used to having modern services and a voice in their destiny as full-fledged members of the United States.

With a population exceeding 128,000, the new decade fostered healthy debates on the statehood issue. The abolishment of fish traps, the need for improved roads and the desire to vote in national elections were among hot topics discussed in cafés, barbershops, garages and meeting rooms across the territory.

Proponents reasoned that statehood would allow Alaska to raise tax revenues and take over management of its fisheries. It also could establish a state-managed police force and state-appointed judiciary. In addition, Alaskans would get two voting members in the U.S. Senate and one in the House of Representatives.

Those in opposition included powerful outside fishing, shipping and mining companies that held monopolies in the territory and flowed profits to the Lower 48. There also were some influential Alaskans who didn't want to change the status quo – including one of the territory's first industrialists.

This political cartoon, drawn by Fairbanks newspaperman Ernest Jessen and possibly appearing in Jessen's Weekly, shows Alaska being carved up by business and governmental interests.

Austin "Cap" Lathrop, who owned the Fairbanks Daily News-Miner, opined that statehood would bring more expenses than the residents could bear. But he had another reason to shun statehood. Lathrop, who owned mines, radio stations, theaters and other businesses in the Last Frontier, didn't want to pay more taxes, which would decrease his profits.

Following Lathrop's accidental death in 1950 at his coal mine in Healy, C.W. "Bill" Snedden took over at the News-Miner. The new publisher endorsed statehood and printed a special supplement dedicated to its merits.

"Give Americans the full privileges of American citizenship," Snedden wrote. "Turn Alaska's destiny over to Alaskans."

Alaska's territorial governor, Ernest Gruening, changed his mind about statehood in the late 1940s. He was opposed to statehood at first and thought it a "mad, wild, and impossible idea that nobody wanted," according to Vide Bartlett in Elizabeth Tower's book about William A. Egan titled, "Alaska's Homegrown Governor."

But Gruening joined statehood advocates after a series of events convinced him that most Alaskans favored it.

Austin "Cap" Lathrop, owner of the Fairbanks Daily News-Miner seen here on Second Street during the 1940s, opposed Alaska becoming a state. After his death in 1950, the new publisher pushed for statehood.

Ernest Gruening, seen here in 1939 taking the oath of office to replace Territorial Gov. John W. Troy, seated, served as Alaska's governor until 1953.

First, Edward Lewis "Bob" Bartlett, running on a statehood platform in 1944, won the right to represent Alaska as the new non-voting delegate to Congress.

Then President Harry S. Truman, in his 1946 State of the Union address, said that statehood should be granted once the federal government knew how Alaskans stood on the issue.

Edward Lewis "Bob" Bartlett, seen here with wife Vide in the 1920s, grew up in Fairbanks and later became known as "the architect of Alaska statehood."

When voters in the territory passed a statewide referendum on statehood by a vote of 9,630 to 6,822 in a special election held later that year, Gruening became a champion for the cause.

Gruening, an Easterner appointed as Alaska's territorial governor from 1939-1953, became convinced that the only way Alaska would get adequate roads, airfields and hospitals, and settle aboriginal rights, was to have elected, voting representatives in Congress.

To that end, he organized a "committee of 100" prominent Americans who supported Alaska's aspirations. Supporters included Eleanor Roosevelt, actor James Cagney and author Pearl S. Buck.

The publisher of the Anchorage Daily Times, Robert B. Atwood, also was a driving force behind making Alaska a state. He contacted publishers across the country and swayed opinion on behalf of statehood.

Atwood, Gruening and a few other concerned citizens met at

Atwood's home in 1946 and formed the Alaska Statehood Association, then created chapters of the organization across the territory.

The association raised money to fund a statehood study. When that study concluded statehood would benefit Alaska, the association made thousands of copies for distribution.

Meanwhile Bartlett, a former gold miner and Fairbanks newspaperman, concentrated on making friends and influencing people in

Robert B. Atwood, left, visits with Vide and Edward Lewis "Bob" Bartlett in the 1950s.

ROAD TO STATEHOOD

Washington, D.C. When he introduced a statehood bill in Congress, it received the first-ever hearing to any bill to make Alaska a state in February 1948.

In one hearing, the head of Alaska Airlines testified about pressure by the salmon industry to keep quiet, or else he would lose their business, according to congressional records.

President Truman, also a statehood supporter, told Congress:

After becoming the territory's official delegate to Congress in 1944, Edward Lewis "Bob" Bartlett, seen here in the 1950s holding a gold bar near Flat, Alaska, worked tirelessly to make Alaska a state.

Alaskans sent postcards, like the one shown here, to people in the Lower 48 in an effort to keep statehood on the minds of the Americans.

"Alaska is our last great frontier area and has the capacity to provide new opportunities for many thousands of our citizens. It contains known resources of food, timber, and minerals of great value to the national economy, and may have much greater resources as yet undiscovered. ...

"I believe, therefore, that we should admit Alaska to statehood at the earliest possible date, and I urge the Congress to enact the necessary legislation. ..."

A subcommittee of the House Committee of Public Lands almost unanimously approved statehood legislation, but the House Rules Committee blocked bringing the bill to the floor before the session adjourned in 1949.

That year, the Territorial Legislature created an official Alaska Statehood Committee. The 11-member group, led by Atwood, dove

A U.S. Senate committee discusses the merits of an Alaska statehood bill in 1950. Note the document near the middle of the table proclaims the territory's "83 years of neglect."

This 1920s political cartoon, drawn by Ernest Jessen, who owned Jessen's Weekly in Fairbanks, shows strings attached to Alaska by federal bureaus anchored to the Capitol Building in Washington, D. C. The issue of federal control of Alaska rang true in 1950, as well.

into convincing national and labor organizations, newspaper editors and state governors to support and publicize Alaska's situation.

"Alaska wants statehood with the fervor men and women give to a transcendent cause," wrote editors of the New York Journal-American. "An overwhelming number of men and women voters in the United States want statehood for Alaska. This Nation needs Alaskan statehood to advance her defense, sustain her security, and discharge her deep moral obligation."

During his 1950 State of the Union address, Truman again urged Congress to enact legislation to make Alaska a state.

A statehood bill did pass the House by a vote of 186-146 but was killed in the Senate by a coalition of conservative Republicans and Southern Democrats – the Republicans feared Alaskans would elect two Democrats to the Senate, tipping the scales of power, and the Southern Democrats feared Alaskan senators would tip the balance on civil rights issues.

The Korean War, which began in June 1950, put the issue of statehood on the nation's back burner for a few more years.

Then the Alaska Territorial Legislature took steps to turn up the heat. On March 22, 1955, it authorized a constitutional convention to draft articles to govern Alaska as a state.

In March 1955, Alaska Territorial Gov. B. Frank Heintzleman signed a bill authorizing a statehood convention to be held at the University of Alaska at College, near Fairbanks, in November. Standing behind the governor, from left: House Minority leader Joseph McLean, Juneau; Senate President James Nolan, Wrangell; House Speaker Wendell Kay, Anchorage; Sen. Earl Cooper, Anchorage; Sen. John Butrovich, Fairbanks; and Rep. Tom Stewart, Juneau.

26

EGAN: THE FINAL PUSH

The man who would become Alaska's first elected state governor had a hand in the territory's march toward statehood. William Allen Egan, born in Valdez in 1914, helped steer the course of the Alaska Constitutional Convention in 1955-1956.

Egan, the godson of Anthony J. Dimond – Alaska's non-voting delegate to Congress from 1932 to 1944 – learned about American politics by faithfully reading the Congressional Record during Dimond's stint in Washington, D.C. He also followed weekly Valdez Miner columns submitted by Dimond's secretary, Edward Lewis "Bob" Bartlett, who became Alaska's delegate in 1944.

Following in his godfather's Democratic Party footsteps, Egan won a seat in the Territorial House of Representatives in 1940. He soon became an avid believer in Dimond's vision of Alaska as a state, which was summarized in an article in the Alaska Frontier in January 1941:

William A. Egan served as a U. S. Army sergeant in World War II.

"Alaska is just as much entitled to statehood as is Hawaii. We'll beat them to it yet if we can. The following steps are necessary to secure a place as the 49th star: (1) presentation by the Territorial Legislature of a petition to Congress voicing the people's request for statehood; (2) passage of an Enabling Act by Congress authorizing the people of Alaska, through a constitutional convention, to draw up a state constitution; (3) submission of this constitution to the people of the Territory, and upon its approval; (4) submission to Congress, whereupon by a resolution of that body, the Territory can be declared to be a State."

The people of Alaska voiced their support for statehood in a 1946 special election, but it took another 14 years for the Alaska Territorial Legislature to authorize a constitutional convention.

William A. Egan served as senator from Valdez in the 21st Territorial Legislature in 1953. This photograph shows presiding Sen. Charles D. Jones of Nome at the desk on the far left, and facing the room are Dora Sweeney, secretary, and Julie Isaac, assistant secretary.

Front row, from left: William L. Lhamon, Fairbanks; Elton Engstrom, Juneau; William A. Egan, Valdez; and William Beltz, Nome.

Second row, from left: A.F. Coble, Fairbanks; John Butrovich, Fairbanks; Mike Stepovich, Fairbanks; Paul Robison, Anchorage; Doris Barnes, Wrangell; Percy Ipalook, Kotzebue; and Curtis Bach, messenger.

Back row, from left: Gerrit Snider, Wasilla; James Nolan, Wrangell; Howard Lyng, Nome; Marcus Jensen, Douglas; and John Gorsuch, Anchorage.

On March 22, 1955, the Territorial Legislature designated November 1955 to begin a 75-day convention to be held on the campus of the University of Alaska in College, near Fairbanks.

Egan, who by this time had been elected to the Territorial Senate, drafted the legislation calling for the convention. As chairman of the Committee on Statehood and National Relations, he worked closely with Rep. Thomas Stewart of Juneau to assure statewide participation in the convention. They settled on 55 delegates to draft a constitution – the same number that wrote the U.S. Constitution in Philadelphia in 1787.

When the group of delegates – 31 from the major cities of Juneau, Fairbanks and Anchorage and 24 from other regions of the territory – gathered at the university on Nov. 8, it included 49 men and six women who were business people, lawyers, miners, fishermen, homemakers and one homesteader. The only Native in the bunch was a Tlingit merchant from Klawok in Southeast Alaska, Frank Peratrovich.

The delegates elected Egan, a merchant who owned a supply store in Valdez and had won an at-large seat, president of the convention. His diplomatic skills, as well as knowledge of parliamentary procedures, proved to be invaluable as the group hammered out the details of what became a 14,400-word document. Peratrovich was chosen as vice chairman.

Former Territorial Gov. Ernest Gruening gave the keynote address the following day to open the convention.

"We meet to validate the most basic of American principles, the principle of consent by the gov-

Delegates elected Frank Peratrovich as vice chairman of the 1955 Constitutional Convention held at the University of Alaska in College, near Fairbanks.

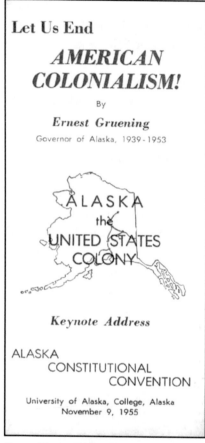

Let Us End

AMERICAN COLONIALISM!

By

Ernest Gruening

Governor of Alaska, 1939-1953

Keynote Address

ALASKA
CONSTITUTIONAL
CONVENTION

University of Alaska, College, Alaska
November 9, 1955

FormerTerritorial Gov.Ernest Gruening gave the keynote address to the Constitutional Convention on Nov. 9, 1955.

erned," Gruening said. "We take this historic step because the people of Alaska who elected you have come to see that their longstanding and unceasing protests against the restrictions, discriminations, and exclusions to which we are subject have been unheeded by the colonialism that has ruled Alaska for 88 years. ..."

On a frigid Feb. 5, 1956, the delegates signed the finished product, which the National Municipal League later called "one of the best state constitutions ever written." It provided for a strong governor, appointed judiciary and a legislature that included 20 senators elected to four-year terms and 40 representatives to serve two-year terms.

It also delayed action on Native land claims, gave the vote to 19-year-olds and declared that resources were to be managed and developed for the benefit of all people.

In a final resolution, the delegates recognized Egan for "... all his parliamentary skill, his unwavering fairness, his personal friendliness, and untiring devotion to duty. ..." They then gave him a portrait of himself painted by artist Christian von Schaedau.

In addition to drafting a constitution, the convention delegates passed two other ordinances to present to Alaskan voters. The first would abolish fish traps and the second, called the Alaska-Tennessee Plan, provided for representation in Washington, D.C.

Alaska Constitution Establishes Boroughs

The framers of Alaska's Constitution found one of their most difficult problems to be the intermediate government between municipalities and the state. Their solution was the creation of a unit known as the "borough."

"It's a county with a New York name," one legislator said.

Most delegates to the Constitutional Convention did not want to slice the territory into a large number of counties as in other states. Valdez delegate William A. "Bill" Egan listed "make-up of the political subdivision" as one of the four major issues to be solved.

And opinions on how to do that ranged widely.

"The issue of the basic composition of local government is a thorny one which must be met," said then-delegate to the U. S. Congress Edward Lewis "Bob" Bartlett when the convention opened.

The problem was turned over to a local government committee led by John Rosswog of Cordova. Serving with him were John Cross of Kotzebue, Victor Fischer and Victor Rivers, both of Anchorage, Eldor Lee of Petersburg, Maynard D. Londborg of Unalakleet and James P. Doogan of Fairbanks.

"The problem is to get a modern local government without duplication, one that will not be burdensome to the people," Rivers said a few weeks later. "The tax structure, for example, should be equitable and overlapping."

The committee called in Vincent Ostrom of Oregon State College to assist in formulating a "workable relationship between the new local government unit and the existing cities within its jurisdiction."

Two days later, the committee recommended the convention "divide the future state into cities and rural municipalities, eliminating counties."

With the new form of government generally conceived, the committee started looking for a name for the unit. While other states used towns, counties, shires, parishes, boroughs and bergs, members of the committee initially felt the identity should be one of Native derivative.

One suggestion combined "nuna," meaning inhabited area, with "puk," which means big, to call the units "nunapuks." But borough eventually won out after much debate.

At its third reading on Jan. 31, 1956, the committee decided that "all local government powers of the State of Alaska shall be vested in boroughs and cities." Approval came only after a vote in which 16 delegates voted for the word "county" and 21 for the word "borough" adopted the local government provision.

As adopted, Article X spelled out "that the entire state shall be divided into boroughs, organized and unorganized," with the legislature to "classify boroughs and prescribe their powers and functions."

There was probably more speculation and less consensus on the future of the borough system under the Alaska Constitution than on any other single subject connected with local government. But the writers of the Alaska Constitution were united on its purpose: "to provide for maximum local self government with a minimum of local government units and duplicating tax-levying jurisdictions."

Alaska Constitutional Convention president, and later governor of Alaska, William A. Egan presided over a meeting of convention delegates at College between November 1955 and February 1956.

The plan, which was used by Tennessee in 1796 to gain admission to the Union, provided for the election of two senators and one representative to send to Congress.

Tennessee, fearing it would never become a state, elected congressional representatives and sent them via horseback to the nation's capital to be recognized as congressmen from the new state of Tennessee. California used the same tactics in 1850 and sent its representatives by stagecoach across the continent to Washington, D.C. Michigan, Iowa, Oregon, Minnesota and Kansas followed similar plans.

On April 24, 1956, Alaska voters approved the constitution by a margin of almost 2-1. They also passed the ban on fish traps and the Alaska-Tennessee Plan. On Oct. 9, they voted for their first U.S. congressmen: Gruening won a senate seat that expired on Jan. 3, 1963; Egan won the senate seat that ended Jan. 3, 1961; and the House of Representative seat, terminating on Jan. 3, 1959, went to Ralph J. Rivers of Fairbanks.

Sen.-elect Egan and Rep.-elect Rivers, along with their wives, left Fairbanks on Dec. 10 for the long trip to the East Coast with Alaska's 15-article constitution in hand.

But instead of traveling by horse or stagecoach like pioneers past, they made their trek using modern horsepower. The newly elected congressmen drove their personal cars, which had been painted white with orange stickers affixed proclaiming Alaska as the 49th state. The Alaska flag also was painted on each door.

Alaska's three prospective congressmen, shown here with their optimistic car sticker, are, from left, Sen.-elect Ernest Gruening, Rep.-elect Ralph Rivers and Sen.-elect William A. Egan. The women are Martha Rivers, left, and Neva Egan. They averaged 300 miles a day on their 1956 trip from Fairbanks to Washington, D.C., used only snow tires with no chains and drove in 60-below-zero temperatures.

Gruening, who now lived in Washington, D.C., occasionally met the motorcade along the route. The trip lasted three weeks and took the Alaska delegation through states that had successfully used the Tennessee Plan to achieve statehood.

After arriving in Washington, D.C., the delegation gave gifts to President Dwight D. Eisenhower and his wife that included smoked salmon, ivory carvings and Arctic Scent cologne.

While the Alaskans were received with great fanfare and applause, they were not recognized or officially seated in Congress that January. Republican legislators didn't want Alaskan Democrats to upset the power balance in Congress, Southern Democrats feared Northern senators would push civil rights issues and many still believed Alaska could not pay for itself.

But a discovery on the Kenai Peninsula late in 1957 began to change those perceptions, and midway through 1958, Egan saw Alaskans' dream of statehood come true.

STATEHOOD AT LAST

27

BLACK GOLD TIPS THE BALANCE

Questions about Alaska's ability to fund its own government lessened when oil-riggers found crude along the Kenai Peninsula in 1957. A Richfield Oil Corp. test well struck black gold at 11,170 feet on July 23. The departure of the first tanker from Swanson River Unit 1, loaded with thousands of barrels of oil bound for California, paralleled the news from Alaska when the *Portland* carried the first load of gold south in 1897.

The 1957 discovery of oil on the Kenai Peninsula began a petroleum boom, including Standard Oil's refinery seen here in Kenai, and helped ensure statehood soon thereafter.

For centuries some Alaska Natives used oil shale in making knives and labrets, similar to this Katalla girl's nose ring.

But this wasn't the first time Alaskans had found oil.

Alaska Natives used the black wealth oozing out of the hills and beaches long before white men found their way north. Eskimos burned the tar-like chips, Southeastern Natives used it for war paint and others used oil shale to make knives and labrets.

The Russians also knew of Alaska Peninsula oil seeps as early as 1860, but since whale oil was the important fuel at the time, oil from rocks was ignored. When the Russian fur trade declined, the Russian American Co. began exploring for minerals while searching for gold only a few miles from the Swanson River oil fields. They passed over the oil and settled for a coal prospect near Kachemak Bay in Cook Inlet.

In 1896, trapper Thomas White was bear hunting in the Controller Bay region near Katalla, about 47 miles southeast of Cordova. While tracking a wounded animal, he fell into thick, black mud seeping up from the ground.

After cleaning his gun and himself, he tossed a match into the pit "to see what would happen," he later said. The pool burst into flames and burned for a month.

It became the first producing oil field discovered in Alaska, and in 1901, the Alaska Development Corp. – known as the English Co. – drilled its first well. It brought in the first gusher the next year at the mouth of the Bering River, about 15 miles from actively producing coalfields. The New York Times printed an overly optimistic report of the find:

"Oil stands in pools and small lakes all over the surface of the lowlands lying east of Copper River ... In places there are lakes of oil covering acres."

The hillside near the discovery site soon blossomed with oil derricks, drilling equipment, cabins and pipelines. Workers dug deep pits in the bog to temporarily store the crude.

Thomas White, center, was known as "The Sourdough Driller" because he drilled the first oil well in Alaska. Also pictured are his wife and son. The man on the left is unidentified.

Above: This is what the first oil tanks looked like in Katalla when crude oil was stored in open pits in the early 1900s.

Below: Front Street in 1904 Katalla is lined with businesses, including The Commerce, Catalla Bar, Board of Trade and Hotel Northern.

Chilkat Oil Co. wells dot the landscape near Katalla during the early 1900s.

Katalla boomed with more than 5,000 people who enjoyed the amenities provided by hotels, banks, stores and a newspaper, the Katalla Herald.

By the fall of 1904, there were 15 holes down or drilling, including two at Katalla, two at Strawberry Harbor and nine between Katalla Slough and the Bering River. About this time the first oil swindle was reported, pulled off by an enterprising prospector. He staked a claim at Controller Bay and sold it for $1,700. When spring breakup came, the claim was carried away – the buyer had purchased a non-sedimentary Controller Bay ice floe.

Katalla had high hopes for oil production. In 1911, a small experimental refinery, the first in Alaska, was built on Katalla Slough a short distance from the oil field and some oil was refined. Expansion of the refinery was accomplished the following year and it went into regular operation, producing gasoline and other products. Most of the refinery products were used in Cordova.

Meanwhile, serious oil exploration had been going on since 1903 in the Alaska Peninsula, with three wells started on the west shore of Cold Bay. But in 1910, the federal government banned oil claims, putting oil on ice until passage of the leasing act of 1920. Until then, with few exceptions, oil activity only occurred in the Katalla field on patented claims.

The Katalla field had produced 56,000 barrels of commercial oil from 10 wells by 1920 – producers ranged from 336 to 1,130 feet deep. Casing head gas was used for power, domestic heat and lighting. Everywhere else, oil production was at a standstill.

The 1920 Mineral Leasing Act ushered in another oil rush. During the first six months of enactment, 178 applications covering 386,673 acres were filed in the Juneau land office. When Alaska had been re-opened to oil seekers, only 40 wells had been drilled in the whole territory, all but nine in the Katalla area. But now there was a renewal of interest in the Alaska Peninsula area. Cold Bay and Kanatak for a brief time were scenes of feverish oil activity and new areas were tested at Yakutat in the Gulf of Alaska.

Cook Inlet and the Matanuska Valley saw renewed interest, too. In 1925, a drilling rig was moved into the Chickaloon area of upper Cook Inlet basin, described as the Lars Netland Cola Lease. Peterson Oil Association began drilling there in spite of advice from geologists that the area wasn't favorable. By 1930, work there dragged to a standstill.

Cook Inlet, now the site of considerable oil activity as seen by this oil-producing unit, claims the distinction of being the site of the first wildcat well in Alaska.

Two men named Pomeroy and Griffen, who formed the Alaska Petroleum Co., had begun drilling at Oil Bay near Iniskin on Cook Inlet in 1898. Oil flow of about 50 barrels was encountered at 700 feet, but at 1,000 feet a flow of water choked off oil production.

The company reorganized as the Alaska Oil Co. and began drilling at Dry Bay in 1902. Tools lost at 320 feet caused the site's abandonment, and a second well was started at Oil Bay in 1904. Little work was done after 1905-1906.

In 1904, there was some trading in acreage in the Upper Inlet, during which options were taken and syndicates organized, but more than 50 years elapsed before the big oil rush came about in this area.

The Chilkat Oil Co. refinery near Katalla, seen here in the 1920s, ceased operations after a fire damaged its boiler house in 1933.

Again oil interest in Alaska dipped. The Chilkat Oil Co. closed its Katalla operations, which had brought in 154,000 barrels in 30 years, after a fire damaged the refinery boiler house on Christmas Day 1933. With the refinery gone, people abandoned the town.

World War II halted oil development by civilians in Alaska, but in the postwar boom years of the 1950s, Alaska began to beckon oil seekers once more.

Phillips Petroleum opened the first oil company office in Anchorage in 1954, and others followed. By the end of 1955, oil companies had leased more than 5 million acres.

The 1957 discovery at Swanson River by Richfield, a small California company that later merged with Atlantic Refining and became ARCO, turned the tide for Alaska crude, and the rush for black gold began in earnest. Two refineries were built, and then more oil was discovered offshore in Cook Inlet in the 1960s.

Cook Inlet oil provided Alaskans with gasoline, diesel fuel, heating oil and jet fuel. And a pipeline, built beneath Turnagain Arm, carried natural gas from the Kenai Peninsula to heat Anchorage homes and businesses.

The giant discovery at Prudhoe Bay on the North Slope in 1968 climaxed more than 60 years of ups and downs of oil exploration in Alaska.

28

WE'RE IN!

At 2 p.m. on June 30, 1958, teletypes and telephones across Alaska began buzzing with exciting news. After six days of debate, the U.S. Senate had voted 64-20 to add Alaska as the 49th state. The House of Representatives already had approved its admission by a vote of 210-166 on May 28.

The long battle for statehood was over.

An Anchorage Daily News headline proclaims statehood on Monday, June 30, 1958.

EXTRA — Anchorage Daily Times — EXTRA

READ BY ALASKANS EVERYWHERE

FORTY-THIRD YEAR — PHONE 48302 — ANCHORAGE, ALASKA, MONDAY, JUNE 30, 1958 — 20 PAGES — PRICE 10 CENTS

WE'RE IN

★★★★★★★ ★★★★★★★ ★★★★★★★ ★★★★★★★ ★★★★★★★ ★★★★★★★ ★★★★★★★

64-20 VOTE MAKES ALASKA 49th STATE

Victory Brings Quick Reactions

Leaders of the Anchorage community could hardly contain their exuberance today as the news came from Washington, D.C., that the Senate had passed the statehood bill.

Reactions ranged the entire gamut of phrases of joy and delight in every phase of Anchorage life.

The sirens blaring out the news that Alaska had become the 49th state drew spectators waiting for the Edna Lee DeMers murder trial to resume out onto the steps of the U.S. courthouse.

Judge J. L. McCarrey Jr., who had just entered the courtroom, adjourned the court. Mrs. DeMers sat in the corridor with her mother, unnoticed as court house employes, lawyers, and visitors surged along the hallways of the courthouse.

In his chambers, minutes later, Judge McCarrey seemed stunned.

He expressed concern over the trend of events. He said he had no comment to make on the passage of statehood. He said only, "My concern is will they allow us to go into this state in an orderly manner."

City Manager George Shannon could only say, "Whoopee! I'm very happy. It means we'll have more home rule. We won't have to go to Washington now for insignificant items of local affairs."

Richard Kennard, president of the Chamber of Commerce, added, "Hallelujah! That's wonderful. I think that's terrific. It's the greatest day of our life."

City Councilman Roy Nigh found he couldn't describe his reaction. "It's wonderful. Words can't describe it." And William Besser, also a councilman, cried out, "Hurrah, I'm delighted."

(Continued on Page 21)

She Goes Up Tonight

BONFIRE CELEBRATION IS TONIGHT

The biggest bonfire in Alaska will be lit tonight to celebrate statehood. Explorer Scouts who have been on guard at the park strip site at Ninth and H will light the fire with torches in an all-out celebration of statehood bill passage by the Senate. The bonfire will spark other similar celebrations throughout Alaska. Forty-nine tons of wood went into the historic pile — with an extra ton for Hawaii. The big celebration at the bonfire will be at 8 p.m. There will be band music, singing, dancing, prayers. Firemen will be on hand to keep the fire under control. Traffic will be kept from the immediate scene. All roads are expected to lead to the park strip for the historic program. This view of the huge pile of wood shows the L Street Apartments in the background.

Anchorage Blows Its Lid

Anchorage blew the lid off today.

Alaska's largest city rocked and rolled as the air was split by the sound of sirens, horns, bells, firecrackers, guns — and everything else that could be used to make a noise.

Sirens sounded first as the official word came through that the Senate had, at long last, passed the statehood bill. Then came the eruption of noise.

Pent-up emotions were released in a spontaneous burst of excitement that penetrated everywhere.

Employes streamed from their places of business and an immediate holiday was declared.

Although most of the activity was uncontrolled, there was some with a definite purpose. Members of the Elks Lodge hurried with their huge American flag to the federal building. There Fur Rendezvous …

(Continued on Page 11)

First 49-Star Flag Goes Up

Within minutes after word was received here of Senate passage of the statehood bill, Federal Electric Corp. claimed it was flying, before anyone else, a flag with 49 stars for the new state. The flag was flying at its Fifth and Barrow building.

Historic Vote Ends 6 Days Of Debate

By A. ROBERT SMITH
Times Washington Correspondent

WASHINGTON (AP) — Alaskan statehood forces won their most historic congressional battle tonight by pushing the statehood bill through the Senate in a whirlwind finish. Opposition forces utterly collapsed tonight after six days of debate.

The historic moment came at 8 o'clock EDT. (2 p.m. Anchorage time). The vote was 64-20. Victory came on the vote of 33 Republicans and 31 Democrats. Opposing it were 12 Democrats and 8 Republicans.

Fighting off all amendments and efforts to sidetrack the bill to a committee for further study, Senator Jackson led statehood backers to the victory they have waited many years to celebrate. At his side throughout the long debate was Alaskan Delegate Bob Bartlett.

The bill now goes to the White House for the signature of President Eisenhower making it the law of the land. This act will trigger the machinery of statehood, allowing Gov. Mike Stepovich to set election dates. After the election, the President will proclaim Alaska the 49th State. The President is expected to sign the bill Wednesday or Thursday and to notify Gov. Stepovich immediately. The governor is in Washington and undoubtedly will be present at the White House to receive the news personally, along with a large contingent of Alaskans who have been in Washington urging passage of the statehood bill.

Final passage came quickly after the defeat of a surprise proposal for sending the bill to the Armed Services Committee 55-31. For an anxious hour or two, this move had statehood backers sweating. It had both Republican and Democratic sponsorship from senators who said they were concerned about national security.

Just before the vote that passed the bill, senators crowded into the chambers, visitors jammed the galleries and there was a feel of history in the making for everyone present. Senators one by one arose to congratulate the many persons in Congress whose efforts were rewarded by tonight's action. When the vote was announced by Senator Neuberger of Oregon, who was presiding at the time, the chamber was filled with applause.

The opposition collapsed after the Senate slapped down an amendment by Sen. Thurmond, 62-22, and followed by shouting down a second Thurmond amendment.

Senator Eastland, the other chief holdout then threw in the sponge and said he wasn't going to even bother to try to send the bill to his Judiciary Committee as he had intended. He said he knew he was licked.

By this time the bandwagon for statehood was rolling in high gear. It had been gathering speed all day in

(Continued on Page 11)

'Great Day' In History Of Alaska

WASHINGTON, (AP) — Senate action, completing Congressional consideration of Alaskan statehood, tonight provoked the following comment:

Delegate E. L. (Bob) Bartlett (D-Alaska) — "This is a great day. This is the greatest day in Alaska's history. The Congress has acted wisely and in the national interest. We of Alaska will justify what has been done this day — we shall make there a state, mighty in every way."

Gov. Mike Stepovich of Alaska:

"Thank God for everything that's happened here. We will show the people of the United States they have not made a mistake."

Territorial Sen. John Butrovich — "It's the American tradition. We've seen it work today."

Sen. William A. Egan, one of Alaska's unofficial Congressional delegation — "Passage of the Alaska statehood bill by the Senate assures that the American citizens of Alaska have won the long fought battle to enjoy their rightful heritage as one of the great states of our America."

(Continued on Page 11)

Anchorage Daily Times typesetter and former Alaska Star editor Lee Jordan had to cut a wooden comma to make the apostrophe for this 6-inch-tall "We're In" headline on June 30, 1958.

STATEHOOD AT LAST

Sirens blared in towns across the territory. Crowds celebrated in the streets. Alaskans had won their 91-year struggle for self-government on June 30, 1958.

Above: When the news of statehood reached the northwestern village of Kotzebue, the town started jumping. Here Laura Mae Beltz goes aloft, via a walrus hide blanket toss, carrying a flag that soon would have a star for her native land. Drummers are, from left, Levi Rexford, Walter Kowunna, Chester Sevek and Charlie Jensen.

Above left: Anchorage Fur Rendezvous Queen Rita Martin, accompanied by a fireman, climbs a fire truck ladder to pin a 49th star on a U.S. flag draped over the Federal Building.

Below left: Jubilant Anchorage residents light a huge bonfire on the Park Strip to celebrate Alaska becoming a state.

In this 1957 political cartoon, it appears that Adlai Stevenson, a leading Democrat in the 1950s, is fishing to make Alaska and Hawaii the 49th and 50th states. With the U.S. Capitol Building in the background, the fisherman holds a net with two state stars in it and wears a hat with a Hawaii fly hooked on. He is landing Alaska in the Fairbanks region.

Following the Constitutional Convention of 1955-1956, which drafted a 14,400-word constitution for the new state, and the efforts of elected representatives through the Alaska-Tennessee Plan, the push for statehood was on. Along with other supporters, like Anchorage Daily Times editor Robert B. Atwood and Alaska-born Territorial Gov. Mike Stepovich, U.S. Sens.-elect Ernest Gruening and William A. Egan and Rep.-elect Ralph J. Rivers joined Alaska's non-voting delegate, Edward Lewis "Bob" Bartlett, on Capitol Hill. The men pounded the halls of Congress for two years, working all angles to get the territory admitted.

There were a few turning points that pushed the cause along.

The appointment of sympathetic Nebraska newspaper publisher Fred Seaton as Secretary of the Interior in 1956 helped sway the opinion of the Eisenhower administration toward statehood. Previously, Eisenhower had endorsed splitting Alaska into two states.

Then a young attorney named Theodore F. "Ted" Stevens arrived on the scene. Stevens, who was U.S. attorney in Fairbanks from 1953 to 1956, was appointed to a position with the Department of Interior under the Eisenhower administration. He became immersed in the statehood issue after C.W. Snedden, publisher of the Fairbanks Daily New-Miner, recommended him to Seaton. Stevens, who became known as "Mr. Alaska" for decades of service as a U.S. senator, served as coordinator of the Alaska and Hawaii statehood movements with the now pro-statehood Secretary of Interior and helped draft the statehood act.

He was instrumental in getting language in the act that persuaded President Dwight D. Eisenhower to support the bill. Eisenhower, who had seen Alaska's value in the defense of the nation during World War II, wanted to keep control of it for military purposes.

Stevens helped draft a provision to give U.S. presidents military powers in Alaska that they don't have in any other state. Section 10 of the Alaska Statehood Act creates a line down the Porcupine and Yukon rivers and on down the Kuskokwim River to the ocean. U.S. presidents can control the land north and west of that line for military defense purposes.

Also, by 1957, Southern senators who had previously opposed admitting both Alaska and Hawaii as states because they feared new senators would not be sympathetic to segregation, knew the tide had turned. Anti-segregation forces already had a clear majority.

And the discovery of a large oil field in the Kenai Peninsula that December proved that Alaska probably would be able to carry its own economic weight.

Prior to heading to the House for a vote, an amendment was added that reduced Alaska's land grant from 183 million to 104 million acres – which was still larger than the state of California. This grant gave Alaska the means to build a solid financial foundation through development or selling of its land.

Once the military and land issues had been worked out, the House and Senate passed the statehood bill. Eisenhower signed the Alaska Statehood Bill into law in private on July 7.

President Dwight D. Eisenhower signs the official papers to make Alaska the 49th state on Jan. 3, 1959. Those watching him sign the document include Vice President Richard M. Nixon, seated left, and the three-man Alaska delegation, standing far left, Ralph Rivers, Ernest Gruening and Edward Lewis "Bob" Bartlett. Anchorage Daily Times editor Robert B. Atwood and former Territorial Gov. Mike Stepovich are standing to the right. The three men standing in the center and the man seated at the right are unidentified.

But Alaska was not officially declared a state until Jan. 3, 1959. The six-month delay was due to payment of salaries for the new state's congressional delegation.

By law, U.S. senators only could receive paychecks for six years at a time. So if Alaska had been admitted following enactment of the statehood bill, it would have caused a financial headache for the payroll people in Washington, D.C., as it would have added unauthorized pay to the new senators' paychecks.

On Aug. 25, 1958, Alaskans showed up in droves to vote in a special election to determine whether the territory would become a state. Three propositions appeared on the ballot, and each needed to pass in order for statehood to be approved.

Statehood Ballot Questions

Proposition No. 1 – "Shall Alaska immediately be admitted into the Union as a State?"

Proposition No. 2 – "The boundaries of the State of Alaska shall be as prescribed in the Act of Congress approved July 7, 1958, and all claims of this State to any areas of land or sea outside the boundaries so prescribed are hereby irrevocably relinquished to the United States."

Proposition No. 3 – "All provisions of the Act of Congress approved July 7, 1958, reserving rights or powers to the United States, as well as those prescribing the terms or conditions of the grants of lands or other property therein made to the State of Alaska, are consented to fully by said State and its people."

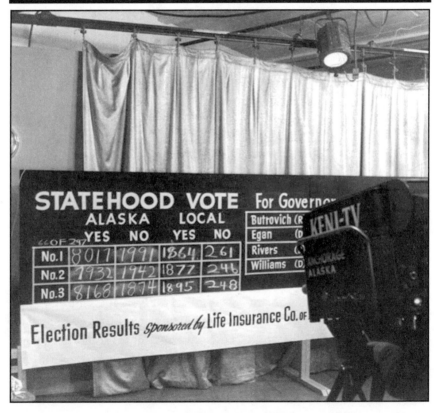

KENI-TV followed the action as votes rolled in during the August 1958 special election for statehood.

Alaska's first elected senate poses for posterity.

By a vote of 6-1, the propositions passed. Voters also determined who would be running to serve as the new state's governor and governing body.

More than 50,000 Alaskans turned out for the general election on Nov. 25. They voted William A. Egan into office as their first elected governor and chose Bartlett and Gruening as the first official senators. Rivers became the first voting representative.

Egan and his lieutenant governor, Hugh Wade, immediately began working with members of the newly elected first state legislature to organize the 49th state's new government. Among their many tasks, they had to create a court system, public works department, fish and game management – one of the state's first acts was to abolish the much-hated use of fish traps – and figure out how to take control of the state's abundant natural resources.

Egan, who had given up his grocery and supply business in

Valdez to serve the people of Alaska, dove into the intricacies of creating a state government. An editorial in the Anchorage Daily Times by Robert B. Atwood, the Democratic governor's former Republican rival, summed up the daunting task that lay ahead.

"The man who wins the governorship gets our sympathy. He will carry the biggest responsibility in establishing the new state government. He must appoint the key men who will operate the agencies of the executive branch. He must appoint the judges of the new state court system. ... The pitfalls for the governor are so numerous that it is frightening. So much depends upon him that a major portion of the fate of the state rests in his hands. ... Policies, rules and procedures must be made that will affect the future as much as the present generation."

Anchorage Daily Times editor Robert B. Atwood holds onto the new 49-star U.S. flag on Jan. 3, 1959. Sharing in the moment are Rep. Ralph Rivers, far left, Sen. Ernest Gruening, third from left beneath the flag, Sen. Edward Lewis "Bob" Bartlett, next to Gruening, and former Territorial Gov. Mike Stepovich, second from right. The other two men are not identified.

The Anchorage Daily Times spread word that Alaska was officially a state on Jan. 3, 1959.

After President Eisenhower signed the paperwork making Alaska statehood official on Jan. 3, Alaskans celebrated again. For the first time since 1912 – when Arizona and New Mexico joined the Union – a new star was added to the U.S. Flag. The 49-star flag only flew for a few months, however, because Hawaii gained statehood on Aug. 21.

After Eisenhower signed the documents that made Alaska a state, Egan took the oath of office to serve and bear the heavy responsibilities associated with creating a new government. But during the ceremony, he already was making plans related to his health.

Egan, who had become ill a month earlier, immediately left for surgery following his swearing in ceremony on Jan. 3. He checked into St. Ann's Hospital in Juneau and underwent surgery to remove his gall bladder and a gallstone.

Instead of recovering, however, his condition worsened.

Wade was appointed acting governor on Jan. 19, and Egan was taken by air to the Virginia Mason Hospital in Seattle. Emergency

Above: Alaska's new governor, William A. Egan, checked into St. Ann's Hospital, seen here in the center behind the Catholic Church in Juneau, for gall bladder surgery on Jan. 3, 1959.

Below: Acting Alaska Gov. Hugh Wade, seated at the desk, meets with, from left,, Sen. William Beltz, of Nome, and two assistants to the governor, Paul Solka and Burke Riley, during 1959.

surgery found a leakage of bile into the abdominal cavity had caused peritonitis. Doctors gave Alaska's first elected governor a 50 percent chance to live.

While Egan did rally, his healing was slow. So the burden of governing fell on Wade's shoulders.

Wade, one of the first group of FBI agents trained by the agency's director, J. Edgar Hoover, in 1925, had traveled extensively across Alaska while he was an agent. The federal government soon recruited him to serve as Alaska director of the National Recovery Administration, based in Juneau. In 1935, he was chosen director of the newly established Social Security Administration and, in 1950, Wade was appointed area director of the Alaska Native Service.

The acting governor and the first elected legislature worked long hours to set up the framework for government during Egan's absence. On April 4, Wade signed the legislature's Reorganization Bill, which allowed the governor to appoint commissioners for 12 established

While recuperating from abdominal surgery at the Virginia Mason Hospital, William A. Egan's wife, Neva, and son, Dennis, seen here with the governor in the late 1950s, visited him in Seattle.

Governor's Mansion

Scott C. Bone, Alaska's territorial governor from 1921-1925, stands in front of the Governor's Mansion in Juneau near the end of his term.

Alaska's first elected governor and his family moved into the mansion in 1959.

The original building, designed by John Knox Taylor, was a 2-1/2 story, 12,900-square-foot frame structure built over a full-size cellar. In the Building Act of 1910, Congress authorized the construction of a dwelling for the governor and appropriated $40,000 to construct and furnish it.

Construction, which began in 1912, was under the direction of William N. Collier, an engineer with the U.S. Treasury Department, which then supervised all public buildings owned by the federal government.

The exterior, completed in 1936, was plastered over with white paint.

The first of nine territorial governors to live in the building was Walter Eli Clark and his family. They hosted the first public function in the residence, a New Year's Open House, on Jan. 1, 1913.

A major internal redesign took place in 1967-1968, which transformed the third floor into two guest suites and one large bedroom.

Another renovation in 1983 included installation of new heating, electrical, plumbing and security systems. It also restored the interior design of the main and second floors to the 1912 era and refinished the original wood floors.

Above: Special license plates were made to identify cars used by the governor and members of Alaska's congressional delegation. Gov. William A. Egan is presented license plate No. 1 by Dana Ingram of the Department of Revenue in 1959.

Below: The U.S. Post Office issued a 7-cent airmail stamp to commemorate Alaska statehood in 1959.

This design for the new 49-star flag didn't make the cut.

departments. Wade then appointed Floyd Guertin as commissioner of administration, a move previously approved by Egan.

Upon Egan's return to duties in the state capital on April 20, Egan wrote Wade a letter of commendation. He also gave the legislature kudos for all it had done in his absence.

"Honestly, the fact that they came up with a balanced budget, while providing the necessary funds for health, welfare, education and the possibility of taking over court system and fisheries, is amazing," he said in an interview with the Daily Alaska Empire. "And don't forget the state reorganization bill. When I left here people were talking about a six-month session and a fall session. There also were no new tax increases passed."

And as it put more pieces of the new government into place, the legislature also adopted a few symbols previously approved by the territorial legislature to represent the new state, including the willow ptarmigan as the state bird, the wild forget-me-not as the official flower and the royal-blue flag with its eight stars of gold, designed by John Ben "Benny" Benson in 1927, as Alaska's flag.

29

'SIMPLE FLAG OF THE LAST FRONTIER'

Alaskans love their flag, designed by half-Aleut John Ben "Benny" Benson in the 1920s. Its simple design of eight stars on a field of blue came from Benson's love of the star-studded skies found in his homeland.

Benson, born in Chignik in 1913, lost his mother when he was 4. His father, a Swedish fox farmer, did not know how to take care of little boys. He put Benny and his brother, Carl, into the Jesse Lee Mission Home, established by Methodist missionaries in 1890 and named for a Methodist preacher.

John Ben "Benny" Benson lived at the Jesse Lee missionary home in Unalaska after his mother died in 1917.

The orphanage, begun by Methodist missionary Agnes Soule and her husband, Dr. Albert Newhall, served the orphans until the home was moved to Seward in 1926.

From the moment Benny moved into the home, missionaries thought there was something special about the serious little boy whose black hair, standing up all over his head, had earned him the nickname "Porcupine."

Benny was a thoughtful youngster, with strangely mature insight even before he was old enough to go to school. One day a missionary who was frying doughnuts rewarded his beseeching dark eyes with one of the golden-brown crullers.

"This doughnut is like you and me, Mrs. Wenchell," he said as he broke the doughnut in two. "It's brown on the outside like me, and white on the inside like you."

The mission home, which was the beginning of Alaska Children's Services, faced many problems in the late teens and early 1920s. The pandemic Spanish influenza that wiped out entire Alaska Native coastal villages during 1918-1919 filled the Unalaska home to overflowing. The home also was old and desperately needed repair, and transportation of children and supplies became unreliable and expensive.

Benny Benson designed Alaska's flag in 1927.

Benny Benson moved in 1926 to the Jesse Lee Home in Seward, pictured here.

In 1926, officials moved the home to the deep-water port of Seward, where larger and more accessible facilities provided children with schooling, job skills and training.

But the orphanage's superintendent, Dr. Albert Newell, could not bring himself to make the move to civilization. He chose to go farther north to Mission in the Arctic. The children, who loved him dearly, had to make the move without him.

One of Benny's last memories of the kind doctor was a prediction Dr. Newell made.

"Benny, some day you're going to be famous," he said.

Many years later, Benny's two little daughters came bursting into the house from school in wide-eyed excitement.

"Daddy, Daddy, we studied about you in school today. You're famous!" they yelled.

Benny felt homesick when he moved to the mainland in 1926, but he soon found that Seward had one great advantage over Unalaska, where thick fog had often obscured the stars overhead. In the town on Resurrection Bay, he had a clear view of the heavens. The youngster went wild with delight and often stayed outdoors in the evenings, star-gazing, dreaming dreams and thinking deep thoughts.

Perhaps his fascination with those distant twinkling stars inspired the 13-year-old Benny when his seventh-grade teacher announced the territory-wide contest for school children to design a flag for Alaska.

The contest was the result of a visit Alaska Territorial Gov. George Parks made in 1925 to the Postmaster General in Washington, D.C. The rotunda of the old post office building was lined with the flags of all the states and territories except Alaska, which had no official flag.

"I'll remedy that," Parks vowed, and announced a flag contest open to all seventh- to 12th-grade students in the territory.

Benny's teacher wrote her pupils' suggestions on the chalkboard as the children's ideas poured out.

"I drew a grizzly bear, first, but it wasn't very good," Benny later told Phyllis Downing Carlson. "Then I looked at the board and saw that one of my suggestions hadn't been used, so I took a piece of 10-by-14 art paper and colored it dark blue. Then I drew on it the seven golden stars of the Big Dipper pointing to the North Star."

In his childish scrawl, he explained his design on his entry.

"The blue field is for Alaska's skies and the forget-me-not, an Alaskan flower. The North Star is for the future state of Alaska, the most northerly of the Union. The Dipper is for the Great Bear, symbolizing strength."

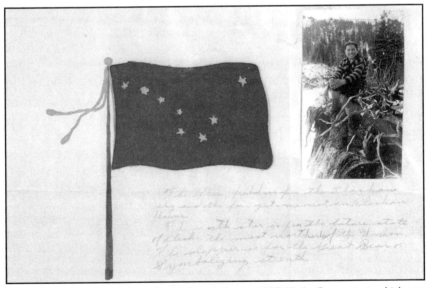

This is the original entry from Benny Benson in the 1927 Alaska flag contest, which garnered 142 designs from Alaska school children in grades 7-12.

From 142 entries, Benny's design was the unanimous choice of the judges.

On April 18, 1927, a telegram was handed to Benny's teacher during school hours. As she read it aloud, Benny grasped his desk and became pale and speechless.

His design had been chosen for Alaska's flag.

His classmates broke into applause.

"Speech, Porcupine, speech," they chanted.

But Benny remained in a trance.

The entire school body was called together,

Benny Benson holds his Alaska flag design at the Jesse Lee Home in Seward in 1927.

and the news was read to all the students. In spite of calls for him to make a speech, all he could do was rise and acknowledge the applause and cheers of his schoolmates.

And even though many honors came to Benny, he kept his humble attitude.

One of his classmates later was quoted in a Christian Science Monitor article:

"Benny is just the same as he was before he got his name in the paper."

The territorial legislature officially adopted Benny's design for Alaska's flag and printed it onto blue silk. It was hoisted into the air for the first time on July 9, 1927, in Juneau.

The young designer received a gold watch with his design engraved on the back and $1,000. He donated the watch to the

Alaska Territorial Gov. George A. Parks, fourth from left, displays the original Alaska flag printed on blue silk in the late 1920s.

Alaska State Museum in 1963, and used the prize money to attend the Hemphill Diesel Engineering School for diesel engine repair in Seattle, Wash.

In 1938, he married Betty Van Hise, and they welcomed their first child, Anna May, that October. Their second daughter, Charlotte Abbot, was born in June 1940. The couple divorced in 1950, and Benny moved with his daughters to Kodiak where he became an airplane mechanic for Kodiak Airways.

Benny's own star rose high, and he received many honors throughout the years. Perhaps his most thrilling moment came when, at the signing of Alaska's Constitution in 1956, he was introduced to the audience as the designer of Alaska's flag.

Those assembled to watch this historic occasion rose to their feet in tumultuous welcome. That once small, motherless Native boy had indeed become famous, an honored member of Alaska's family, and one of its most respected, best-loved citizens.

His skies weren't always cloudless, though. He suffered frostbite

Benny Benson, Gov. William A. Egan and Benson's daughter, Charlotte, hold a framed replica of Benny's Alaska flag design in the late 1950s.

during the early 1960s, which plagued him with poor circulation. In 1966, doctors amputated one of his toes. But he didn't let that slow him down.

"Now I have one less toenail to trim," he joked.

A bad fall in 1969 did get him down for a bit, however, as it led to amputation of his right leg above the knee.

"I'll be able to get around with an artificial leg," he said. "I'll be almost as good as ever.

Benny kept busy sewing custom, autographed Alaska flags for legislators, dignitaries and each Miss Alaska.

While he kept his eyes on the North Star and the seven golden stars of the Great Dipper, his design mingled with the real constellations in July 1969. Benny's flag, together with the flags of the other 49 states, landed on the moon, deposited there by crewmembers of Apollo 11 – the first astronauts to set foot on the moon's surface.

Benny Benson, the only living state flag designer at the time, saw

Alaska's flag joined those of the other 49 states aboard the Apollo 11 mission to the moon in July 1969.

the flag that took him on that long trip from obscurity to fame, taken itself, thousands of miles through space on perhaps the most historic voyage in history.

He died of a heart attack three years later on July 2, 1972. He was 58.

But Alaskans have an endearing memory of the boy from the Bush who gave them something they love and cherish – 'the simple flag of the Last Frontier.'

Alaska's Flag
Words by Marie Drake

Eight stars of gold on a field of blue —
Alaska's flag, May it mean to you
The blue of the sea, the evening sky,
The mountain lakes, and the flow'rs nearby;
The gold of the early sourdough's dreams,
The precious gold of the hills and streams;
The brilliant stars in the northern sky,
The "Bear"— the "Dipper" — and,
Shining high,
The great North Star with its steady light,
Over land and sea a beacon bright,
Alaska's flag — to Alaskans dear,
The simple flag of a last frontier.

Marie Drake, below left, wrote the poem that became "Alaska's Flag," the state song, in the mid-1930s. As assistant commissioner of education for the territory, she edited and wrote most of the material for the department's School Bulletin. The poem first appeared on the cover of the bulletin's October 1935 issue.

In recognition of her devotion to the young people of Alaska, Drake received an honorary Doctor of Letters degree from the University of Alaska in 1958. She died March 5, 1963.

Elinor Dusenbury, below right, created the melody for the poem in 1940, and the Territorial Legislature adopted "Alaska's Flag" as Alaska's official song in 1955.

Upon learning that the U.S. House of Representatives had voted on May 28, 1958, to admit Alaska as the 49th state in the Union, Gov. William A. Egan's wife, Neva, sang "Alaska's Song" to a group gathered in the Senate chapel in Washington, D.C., according to Elizabeth A. Tower in her book, "Alaska's Homegrown Governor."

Franklin Bulte is at the piano in this 1950s photo taken during a song-signing in Juneau.

BIBLIOGRAPHY

Alaska Geographic Society. *Alaska's Oil/Gas & Minerals Industry.*
Edmonds, WA: Alaska Geographic Society, 1982.

Andrews, Clarence L. *The Story of Alaska.* Caldwell, ID: Caxton
Printers Ltd., 1947.

Antonson, Joan M. and Hanable, William S. *Alaska's Heritage.*
Anchorage, AK: Alaska Historical Commission, 1985.

Atwood, Evangeline. *Frontier Politics: Alaska's James Wickersham.*
Portland, OR: Binford and Mort, 1979.

Barry, Mary J. *A History of Mining on the Kenai Peninsula, Alaska.*
Anchorage, AK: MJP BARRY, 1997.

Bezeau, M.V. *Strategic Cooperation: The Canadian Commitment to the
Defense of Alaska in the Second World War. In Alaska at War, 1941-1945,*
edited by Fern Chandonnet. Anchorage, AK: Alaska at War
Committee, 1995.

Borneman, Walter R. *Alaska: Saga of a Bold Land.* New York, NY:
HarperCollins, 2003.

Bowkett, Gerald. *Reaching for a Star.* Fairbanks, AK: Epicenter
Press, 1989.

Brooks, Alfred Huse. *Blazing Alaska's Trails.* Fairbanks, AK: University
of Alaska Press, 1973.

Brown, Earl L. ed. *Alcan Trail Blazers: Alaska Highway's Forgotten Heroes.*
Fort Nelson, BC: Autumn Images, 2005.

Bush, James D. Jr. *Narrative Report of Alaska Construction, 1941-1944.*
Anchorage, AK: Alaska Defense Command, 1943.

Carberry, Michael, and Lane, Donna. *Patterns of the Past, An Inventory of
Anchorage's Historic Resources.* Anchorage, AK: Van Cleve Printing
Co., 1986.

Case, David S. *Alaska Natives and American Laws.* Fairbanks, AK:
University of Alaska Press, 1984.

Cloe, John Haile. *The Aleutian Warriors: A History of the 11th Air Force and
Fleet Air Wing 4.* Missoula, MT: Pictorial Histories Publishing Co. Inc.
and Anchorage Chapter Air Force Association, 1990.

Cohan, Stan. *ALCAN and CANOL: A Pictorial History of Two Great
World War II Construction Projects.* Missoula, MT: Pictorial Histories
Publishing, 1992.

Cohen, Stan. *Flying Beats Work: The Story of Reeve Aleutian Airways.*
Missoula, MT: Pictorial Histories Pub., 1988.

Cole, Terrence. *The Capture of Attu: Tales of World War II in Alaska, as
Told by the Men who Fought There.* Anchorage, AK: Alaska Northwest
Publishing, 1984.

Corbett, Helen D. and Swibold, Susanne M. *The Aleuts of the Pribilof Islands, Alaska, Endangered Peoples of the Arctic: Struggles to Survive and Thrive.* Ed. Milton M.R. Freeman, Westport, CT: Greenwood Press, 2000.

Daniels, Roger, et al., ed. *Japanese Americans from Relocation to Redress.* Revised edition, Seattle, WA: University of Washington Press, 1986.

Day, Beth. *Glacier Pilot.* Sacramento, CA: Comstock Publishing, 1976.

Denfeld, Colt D. *The Defense of Dutch Harbor, Alaska from Military Construction to Base Cleanup.* Anchorage, AK: U.S. Army Corps of Engineers, 1987.

Doolittle, General James H., with Glines, Carroll V. *I Could Never Be So Lucky Again.* New York, NY: Bantam Books, 1991.

Driscoll, Joseph. *War Discovers Alaska.* Philadelphia, PA: Lippincott, 1943.

Fischer, Victor. *Alaska's Constitutional Convention.* Fairbanks, AK: University of Alaska Press, 1975.

Fitch, Edwin M. *The Alaska Railroad.* New York, NY: Frederich A. Praeger Publishers, 1967.

Fortuine, Robert. *Must We All Die? Alaska's Enduring Struggle with Tuberculosis.* Fairbanks, AK: University of Alaska Press, 2005.

Fortuine, Robert. *Chills and Fever: Health and Disease in the Early History of Alaska.* Fairbanks, AK: University of Alaska Press, 1992.

Freeman, Elmer A. *Those Navy Guys and Their PBY's: The Aleutian Solution.* Spokane, WA: Kedging Publishing Co., 1984.

Garfield, Brian. *The Thousand-Mile War: World War II in Alaska and the Aleutians.* Revised edition, Fairbanks, AK: University of Alaska Press, 1995.

Gilman, William. *Our Hidden Front.* New York, NY: Reynal and Hitchcock, 1944.

Glines, Carroll V. *Doolittle's Tokyo Raiders.* New York, NY: Van Nostrand Reinhold Co., 1981.

Griffin, Harold. *Alaska and the Canadian Northwest: Our New Frontier.* New York, NY: Norton, 1944.

Griggs, William E. (photographer), Merrill, Philip J. (editor). *The World War II Black Regiment That Built the Alaska Military Highway: A Photographic History.* Jackson, MS: University Press of Mississippi, 2002.

Gruening, Ernest. *An Alaskan Reader.* New York, NY: Meredith Press, 1966.

Gruening, Ernest. *Many Battles: The Autobiography of Ernest Gruening.* New York, NY: Liveright, 1973.

Gruening, Ernest. *The Battle for Alaska Statehood.* Fairbanks, AK: University of Alaska Press. 1967.

Gruening, Ernest. *The State of Alaska.* New York, NY: Random House, 1954.

Haycox, Stephen. *Alaska: An American Colony.* Seattle, WA: University of Washington Press, 2002.

BIBLIOGRAPHY

Haycox, Stephen W. and Mangusso, Mary Childers. *An Alaska Anthology: Interpreting the Past*. Seattle, WA: University of Washington Press, 1996.

Hays, Otis E. Jr. *The Alaska-Siberia Connection: The World War II Air Route*. Texas A&M University Military History Series, 48, College Station, TX: Texas A&M University Press, 1996.

Hillel, Shlomo. *Operation Babylon*. Translated by Ina Friedman, Garden City, NY: Doubleday, London: Collins, 1987.

Hulley, Clarence C. *Alaska Past and Present*. Portland, OR: Binfords & Mort, 1953.

Hunt, William R. *Alaska: A Bicentennial History*. New York, NY: W.W. Norton, 1976.

Kirkland, John C. *The Relocation and Internment of the Aleuts during World War II, 8 vol*. Anchorage, AK: Aleutian/Pribilof Islands Association, 1981.

MacLean, Robert Merrill, and Rossiter, Sean. *Flying Gold: The Adventures of Russell Merrill, Pioneer Alaskan Aviator*. Fairbanks, AK: Epicenter Press, 1994.

Marston, Marvin R. *Men of the Tundra: Alaska Eskimos at War*. New York, NY: October House, 1969.

Mills, Stephen E. *Arctic War Planes: Alaska Aviation of World War II: A Pictorial History of Bush Flying with the Military in the Defense of Alaska and America*. New York, NY: Bonanza Books, 1978.

Mills, Stephen E., and Phillips, James W. *Sourdough Sky*. Seattle, WA.: Superior Publishing Co., 1969.

Mitchell, Donald Craig. *Sold American: The Story of Alaska Natives and Their Land, 1867-1959*. Fairbanks, AK: University of Alaska Press, 2003.

Morenus, Richard. *Alaska Sourdough: The Story of Slim Williams*. Stokie, IL: Rand McNally, 1968.

Morison, Samuel Eliot. *Aleutians, Gilberts and Marshalls, June 1942-April 1944, vol. 7 of History of United States Naval Operations in World War II*. Champaign, IL: University of Illinois Press, 2001.

Naske, Claus M. *A History of Alaska Statehood*. Lanham, MD: University Press of America, 1985.

Naske, Claus M. and Slotnick, Herman E. *Alaska, A History of the 49th State*. Grand Rapids, MI: William E. Eerdmans Publishing Co., 1979

Naske, Claus M. and Ludwig J. Rowinski. *Anchorage, A Pictorial History*. Norfolk, VA: Donning, 1981.

Naske, Claus M. *An Interpretative History of Alaskan Statehood*. Anchorage, AK: Alaska Northwest Publishing Co., 1973.

Naske, Claus M. *Edward Lewis Bob Bartlett of Alaska: A Life in Politics*. Fairbanks, AK: University of Alaska Press, 1979.

Nelson, Arnold G. and Helen Nelson. *The Bubble of Oil at Katalla*. The Alaska Journal, a 1981 Collection. Anchorage, Alaska: Alaska Northwest Publishing Co., 1981.

Nielson, Jonathan M. *Armed Forces on a Northern Frontier: The Military in Alaska's History*. New York, NY: Greenwood, 1988.

Potter, Jean. *Alaska Under Arms*. New York, NY: Macmillan Co., 1942.

Potter, Jean. *Flying Frontiersmen*. New York, NY: MacMillan Co., 1956.

Price, Kathy. *The World War II Heritage of Ladd Field, Fairbanks, Alaska*. Ft. Collins, CO: Center for Environmental Management of Military Lands, Colorado State University, 2004.

Rearden, Jim. *Castner's Cutthroats: Saga of the Alaska Scouts*. Prescott, AZ: Wolfe Publishing, 1990.

Rearden, Jim. *Koga's Zero: The Fighter that Changed World War II*. Missoula, MT: Pictorial Histories Publishing, 1995.

Rimley, David. *Crooked Road: The Story of the Alaska Highway*. New York, NY: McGraw Hill Book Co., 1976.

Rourke, Norman E. *War Comes to Alaska: The Dutch Harbor Attack, June 3-4, 1942*. Shippensburg, PA: White Mane Publishing Co., 1997.

Salisbury, C.A. *Soldiers of the Mists: Minutemen of the Alaska Frontier*. Missoula, MT: Pictorial Histories Publishing, 1992.

Scheffer, Victor B. *The Year of the Seal*. New York, NY: Charles Scribner and Sons, 1970.

Sherwood, Morgan. *Alaska and Its History*. Seattle, WA: University of Washington Press, 1967.

Sicron, Moshe. *Immigration to Israel 1948-1953*. Jerusalem: Falk Project for Economic Research in Israel, 1957.

Skinner, Ramona Ellen. *Alaska Native Policy in the Twentieth Century*. New York, NY: Garland Publishing, 1997.

Sparkz, India M. *Eight stars of gold: the story of Alaska's flag*. Alaska State Museum, 2001.

Thomas, Lowell and Jablonski, Edward. *Bomber Commander: The Life of James H. Doolittle*. London: Sidgwick & Jackson, 1976.

Sterling, Robert J. *Character & Characters: The Spirit of Alaska Airlines*. Seattle, WA: Documentary Media LLC, 2008.

Szurovy, Geza. *Bushplanes*. St. Paul, MN: Zenith Imprint, 2004.

Torrey, Barbara Boyle. *Slaves of the Harvest: The Story of the Pribilof Aleuts*. St. Paul, AK: Tanadgusix Corp., 1978.

Tower, Elizabeth A. *Anchorage, City History Series*. Seattle, WA: Epicenter Press, 1999.

Tower, Elizabeth A. *Alaska's Homegrown Governor*. Anchorage, AK: E. A. Tower, 2003.

Twichell, Heath. *Northwest Epic: The Building of the Alaska Highway*. New York, NY: St. Martin's Press, 1992.

Van Tuyll, Hubert P. *Feeding the Bear: American Aid to the Soviet Union, 1941–1945*. New York, NY: Greenwood Press, 1989.

Wachel, Pat and Winchell, Oscar. *Alaska's Flying Cowboy*. Minneapolis, MN: T. S. Denison and Co. Inc., 1967.

Weeks, Albert Loren. *Russia's Lifesaver: Lend-lease Aid to the U.S.S.R. in World War II*. Lanham, MD: Lexington Books, 2004.

Wickersham, Hon. James. *Old Yukon*. Washington, DC: Washington Law Book Company, 1938.

Government sources

Alaska Bureau of Vital Statistics, 1998 Annual Report.

Alaska Department of Fish and Game, Sustaining Alaska's Fisheries: Fifty Years of Statehood.

Alaska Department of Health and Social Services, Middaugh J, Miller J, Dunaway C et al. Causes of Death in Alaska: 1950, 1980-89. Section of Epidemiology.

Alaska State Library, Personal diaries of James Wickersham.

Parran T, et al: Alaska's Health: A Survey Report to the United States Department of the Interior. Graduate School of Public Health, University of Pittsburgh, 1954.

Reynolds, G.L. Historical Overview and Inventory: White Alice Communications System, Elmendorf AFB, AK: Prepared for the U.S. Air Force Alaskan Air Command, 1988.

Schaffel, K. The Emerging Shield: The Air Force and the Evolution of Continental Air Defense 1945-1960, Washington, DC: Office of Air Force History, 1991.

Sitka National Historic Park, Anonymous. Siems Drake Puget Sound, The Story of Alaska's Naval Air Bases in World War II. Typescript.

Unalaska High School, Aleutian Invasion: World War Two in the Aleutian Islands. Prepared by the students of Unalaska High School. Unalaska, 1981

U.S. Department of Interior, Geological Survey 1951, Preliminary Report on the Geology and Oil Possibilities of the Katalla District, Alaska.

U.S. Department of Interior, National Park Service, Elmendorf Air Force Base, Vol. 1, Historic Context of World War II Buildings and Structures.

U.S. Department of Interior, National Park Service, War and Evacuation in Alaska, Personal Justice Denied, Report of the Commission on Wartime Relocation and Internment of Civilians

U.S. Government Printing Office, Guarding the United States and Its Outposts, The Western Hemisphere, United States Army in World War II.

U.S. Government Printing Office, The Army's Role in the Building of Alaska. Pamphlet 360-5.

U.S. Government Printing Office, The Corps of Engineers: The War Against Japan. The Technical Services. United States Army in World War II.

U.S. Navy, Bureau of Yards and Docks. Building the Navy's Bases in
    World War II, 2 vols.
U.S. Navy, The Aleutians Campaign, June 1942-August 1943.
    Washington: Naval Historical Center, Department of the Navy, 1993.

Periodicals and Newspapers

Anchorage Daily News, June 30, 1958
Anchorage Daily News, Aug. 15, 1958
Anchorage Daily News, Aug. 27, 1958
Anchorage Daily News, Dec. 1, 1958
Anchorage Daily News, Dec. 26, 1958
Anchorage Daily News, May 12, 1980
Anchorage Daily News, July 16, 2008
Anchorage Daily Times, Jan. 21, 1938
Anchorage Daily Times, July 22, 1940
Anchorage Daily Times, Jan. 3, 1959
Alaska Frontier, January 1941
Alaska Geographic Society, Vol. 9, 1982
Alaska Journal 2, 1981
Alaska Journal 14, 1984
Alaska Journal 16, 1986
Alaska Magazine, May 1976
Alaska Magazine, September 1986
Alaska Magazine, May-December 2008
Air Transport World, Alaska Airlines, December 2007
Business Wire, May 2001
CHEST, 1940, Vol. 6
Greatlander Shopping News, Nov. 22, 1978
International Journal of Circumpolar Health, 1998
Military Engineer, Jan.-Feb. 1941
National Geographic Magazine, Feb. 1943
Nome Nugget, April 1942
Pacific Northwest Quarterly, 74, 1983
Petroleum News Alaska, 1997
Seattle Times, March 4, 1951
The Daily Alaska Empire, Feb. 6, 1945
The New York Times, March 22, 1880
The New York Times, July 3, 1983
Western Historical Quarterly, April 1980

Personal Communications
Bruce D. Merrell, Alaska bibliographer, ZJ Loussac Public Library
John P. Bagoy, Anchorage historian
John Benny Benson interview w/Phyllis Carlson 1960s

Web sites
Alaska History & Cultural Studies, @ www.akhistorycourse.org
Alaska Railroad, U.S. Department of Interior, @ www.alaskarails.org
Aleutian Campaign 1942-1943, USAF Museum
    @ www.wpafb.af.mil/museum/history
American Experience/Building the Alaska Highway, Public Broadcasting
System @ pbs.org
Eklutna project, U.S. Bureau of Reclamation
    @ www.usbr.gov/history/eklutna
E.L. Bartlett, The Architect of Alaska Statehood
    @ xroads.virginia.edu/~cap/BARTLETT
Elizabeth Peratrovich Day, State of Alaska
    @ www.gov.state.ak.us/archive-49150.html
Elmendorf Air Force Base military history
    @www.elmendorf.af.mil/library
Harry S. Truman Library and Museum @ www.trumanlibrary.org
History of Alaska Airlines, Alaska Airlines @ www.alaskaair.com
James H. Doolittle, U.S. Air Force biography @ www.af.mil/news
Lit Site Alaska, University of Alaska Anchorage, @ www.litsite.org
Statehood, Channel 2 News @ www.ktuu.com
Sydney Laurence Website @ www.sydneylaurence.com
U.S. Army Center of Military History @ www.history.army.mil
World War II In The Aleutians @ www.hlswilliwaw.com/aleutians

PHOTO CREDITS

FOREWORD
P.7, Aunt Phil's Files; P.8, top, University of Alaska Anchorage, National Geographic Society Katmai Expeditions Collection, UAA-hmc-0186-volume6-H138; P.8, bottom, University of Alaska Anchorage, Edwin Forbes Glenn Collection, UAA-hmc-0116-series3a-32-1; P.11, Seward Community Library, SCL-1-798.

CHAPTER 1: DEFENSE FOR ALASKA
P.14, U.S. National Archives, 80-G-16871; P.15, U.S. National Archives, 80-G-32420; P.16, Alaska State Library, Place File, ASL-Haines-PortChilkoot-10; P.17, University of Alaska Anchorage, John Carroll Benton World War II, UAA-hmc-0645-29b; P.18, University of Alaska Anchorage, George K. Steve Brodie, UAA-hmc-0378-series2-1b; P.20a, University of Alaska Anchorage, Zenas Richard World War II Album, UAA-hmc-0548-31c, P.20b, University of Alaska Fairbanks, Kay J. Kennedy Aviation Collection, UAF-1991-98-869.

CHAPTER 2: RUSSIA'S SECRET MISSION
P.21, University of Alaska Fairbanks, Kay J. Kennedy Aviation Collection, UAF-1991-98-867; P.22, University of Alaska Fairbanks, Candace Waugaman Collection, UAF-2005-123-7; P.23, Anchorage Museum of History & Art, General Photograph File, AMRC-b95-12-5; P.24, University of Alaska Fairbanks, Kay J. Kennedy Aviation Collection, UAF-1991-98-837; P.25, University of Alaska Fairbanks, Kay J. Kennedy Aviation Collection, UAF-1991-98-840; P.26, University of Alaska Fairbanks, Kay J. Kennedy Aviation Collection, UAF-1991-98-851; P.27, University of Alaska Fairbanks, Kay J. Kennedy Aviation Collection, UAF-1991-98-861; P.28a, Anchorage Museum of History and Art, Wien Collection, AMRC-b85-27-1204; P.28b, University of Alaska Fairbanks, Kay J. Kennedy Aviation Collection, UAF-1991-98-868; P.29a, University of Alaska Fairbanks, Kay J. Kennedy Aviation Collection, UAF-1991-98-865; P.29b, University of Alaska Fairbanks, Kay J. Kennedy Aviation Collection, UAF-1991-98-850; P.30, University of Alaska Fairbanks, Kay J. Kennedy Aviation Collection, UAF-1991-98-866; P.31, University of Alaska Fairbanks, Kay J. Kennedy Aviation Collection, UAF-1991-98-870; P.32a, University of Alaska Fairbanks, Kay J. Kennedy Aviation Collection, UAF-1991-98-845; P.32b, Alaska State Library, The Army in Alaska, ASL-P008-28.

CHAPTER 3: ARMY BASE REVITALIZES ANCHORAGE
P.33, University of Alaska Anchorage, American Museum of Natural History, Alaska-Yukon Expedition, UAA-hmc-0600-19b; P.34 University of Alaska Anchorage, Thomas Culhane, UAA-hmc-0096-series2-1-63-2; P.35, Aunt Phil's Files; P.36, University of Alaska Anchorage, Russell W. Dow, UAA-hmc-0396-14f-713; P.37a, University of Alaska Anchorage, Russell W. Dow, UAA-hmc-0396-14f-192; P.37b, University of Alaska Anchorage, Russell W. Dow, UAA-hmc-0396-14f-732; P.38a, Anchorage Museum of History and Art, General Photograph File, AMRC-b72-88-17; P.38b, University of Alaska Anchorage, Archives & Special Collections, Marie Silverman, APU Collection, UAA-hmc-0778-6-40; P.39, Alaska State Library, U.S. Army Signal Corps, ASL-P175-105; P.40, Anchorage Museum of History & Art, General Photograph File, AMRC-b67-23-54; P.41, Anchorage Museum of History

& Art, General Photograph File, AMRC-b65-18-569; P.42, University of Alaska Fairbanks, William A. Egan Papers, UAF-1985-120-97; P.43, Courtesy U.S. Air Force; P.44a, Anchorage Museum of History and Art, General Photograph File, AMRC-b65-2-17; P.44b, University of Alaska Anchorage, George F. Rickey, UAA-hmc-0505-115; P.45, University of Alaska Anchorage, Russell W. Dow, UAA-hmc-0396-14f-62.

CHAPTER 4: RAILROADER TUNNELS TO WHITTIER
P.47, Alaska State Library, Mary Nan Gamble, ASL-P270-843; P.48, Courtesy National Park Service; P.49, Courtesy Alaska Railroad Corp.; P.50a, University of Alaska Fairbanks, Cecil H. Kornegay, UAF-1999-204-25; P.50b, Anchorage Museum of History and Art, John Urban Collection, AMRC-b64-1-676;

CHAPTER 5: ROAD HEADS NORTH TO ALASKA
P.52, Courtesy National Park Service; P.53, Alaska State Library, Alaska Highway Construction, ASL-P193-024a; P.54, Anchorage Museum of History & Art, Crary-Henderson Collection, AMRC-b62-1-938; P.55, University of Iowa Libraries, Special Collections Department, Redpath Chautauqua Collection; P.56, Courtesy Library of Congress; P.57, Courtesy Bureau of Land Management; P.58, University of Alaska Anchorage, Christine M. McClain Papers, UAA-hmc-0370-series15a-1-80; P.59, University of Alaska Fairbanks, Donald Parker Collection, UAF-1933-194-28; P.60, Alaska State Library, Alaska Highway Construction, ASL-P193-156a; P.61, University of Alaska Fairbanks, James Monroe (Pat) James, UAF-2004-92-1; P.62, Alaska State Library, Alaska Highway Construction, ASL-P193-151; P.63, Courtesy Library of Congress; P.64a, Alaska State Library, Alaska Highway Construction, ASL-P193-001; P.64b, Alaska State Library, Alaska Highway Construction, ASL-P193-002; P.65a, Alaska State Library, Alaska Highway Construction, ASL-P193-008; P.65b, University of Alaska Fairbanks, James Monroe (Pat) James, UAF-2004-92-16; P.66, Courtesy National Archives; P.67, Alaska State Library, Alaska Highway Construction, ASL-P193-023; P.68a, Alaska State Library, Alaska Highway Construction Photograph, ASL-P193-034; P.68b, Alaska State Library, Alaska Highway Construction, ASL-P193-193; P.69a, Courtesy Library of Congress; P.69b, Alaska State Library, Alaska Highway Construction, ASL-P193-191; P.70, University of Alaska Fairbanks, James Monroe, UAF-2004-92-15; P.71a, Alaska State Library, Alaska Highway Construction, ASL-P193-158; P.71b, University of Alaska Fairbanks, Donald Parker Collection, UAF-1993-194-69; P.72a, Alaska State Library, Alaska Highway Construction, ASL-P193-044; P.72b, Alaska State Library, Alaska Highway Construction, ASL-P193-047; P.73a, Alaska State Library, Alaska Highway Construction, ASL-P193-022; P.73b, Alaska State Library, Alaska Highway Construction, ASL-P193-040; P.74a, Anchorage Museum of History and Art, General Photograph File, AMRC-b76-168-9; P.74b, Courtesy Library of Congress; P.75, Alaska State Library, Fred B. Dodge, ASL-P42-100; P.76, Courtesy Library of Congress; P.77, University of Alaska Fairbanks, James Monroe (Pat) James, UAF-2004-92-5; P.78a, University of Alaska Anchorage, Christine M. McClain Papers, UAA-hmc-0370-series15a-3-64; P.78b, Anchorage Museum of History and Art, General Photograph File, AMRC-b74-4-19.

CHAPTER 6: OUTPOSTS SPRING UP
P.79, Aunt Phil's Files; P.80, University of Alaska Anchorage, Hans and Margaret Hafemeister

Papers, UAA-hmc0126-m1-238; P.81, University of Alaska Fairbanks, Ernest H. Gruening Papers, UAF-1976-21-55361; P.82a, Alaska State Library, H. Marion Thornton, ASL-P338-1567; P.82b, Alaska State Library, H. Marion Thornton, ASL-P338-1642; P.83, University of Alaska Fairbanks, San Francisco Call-Bulletin, UAF-1970-11-93; P.84, University of Alaska Anchorage, John Carroll Benton, UAA-hmc-0645-41c; P.85a, Alaska State Library, Richard G. and Mary S. Culbertson Collection, ASL-P390-094; P.85b, University of Alaska Anchorage, John Carroll Benton World War II Collection, UAA-hmc-0645-33c; P.86, Aunt Phil's Files; P.87a, Alaska State Library, James S. Russell, ASL-P98-45; P.87b, University of Washington, John E. Thwaites, THW334; P.88a, University of Alaska Fairbanks, American Japanese Joint Expedition 1967, UAF-2006-131-172; P.88b, University of Alaska Fairbanks, Walter W. Hodge Papers, UAF-2003-63-204; P.89a, Alaska State Library, James S. Russell, ASL-P98-41; P.89b, Alaska State Library, U.S. Alaska Communication System, ASL-P64-0990; P.90a, Alaska State Library, Dora M. Sweeney, ASL-P421-294; P.90b, Alaska State Library, Dora M. Sweeney, ASL-P421-291; P.91, Alaska State Library, U.S. Army Signal Corp, ASL-P175-116; P.92a, Alaska State Library, U.S. Army Signal Corp, ASL-P175-119; P.92b, Alaska State Library, U.S. Army Signal Corp, ASL-P175-114; P.93a, University of Alaska Anchorage, J.B. "Georgia" Harper, UAA-hmc-0592-20c; P.93b, Anchorage Museum of History and Art, Crary-Henderson Collection, AMRC-b62-1-a-148; P.94a, University of Alaska Anchorage, Lawrence E. Marx, Nome Air Base Collection, UAA-hmc-0581-4; P.94b, Seward Community Library, DC Brownell Collection, SCL-28-8; P.95a, Seward Community Library, Jesse Lee Home, SCL-7-3; P.95b, University of Alaska Anchorage, Robert C. Lewis Papers, UAA-hmc-0015-series2-3-3; P.96, Alaska State Library, J. Simpson MacKinnon, ASL-P80-076; P.97a, University of Alaska Anchorage, Russell W. Dow, UAA-hmc-0396-14f-192; P.97b, University of Alaska Anchorage, Russell W. Dow, UAA-hmc-0396-14f-175; P.98a, Anchorage Museum of History & Art, General Photograph File, AMRC-b80-168-15; P.98b, Alaska State Library, James S. Russell, ASL-P98-46; P.99, Alaska State Library, U.S. Army Signal Corps, ASL-P175-095.

CHAPTER 7: ESKIMO SCOUTS VOLUNTEER

P.100, Alaska State Library, Mabel and Emil Fisher, ASL-P368-89; P.101, Alaska State Library, Trevor M. Davis, ASL-P97-0010; P.102, University of Alaska Fairbanks, William A. Egan Papers, UAF-1985-120-98; P.103, University of Alaska Fairbanks, Ernest H. Gruening Papers, UAF-1976-21-571; P.104a, University of Alaska Anchorage, Howard and Mabel Jonish Papers, UAA-hmc-0428-series5-f1-6; P.104b, Alaska State Library, Dr. Daniel S. Neuman, ASL-P307-0214; P.105, University of Alaska Fairbanks, Ernest H. Gruening Papers, UAF-1976-21-587; P.106, University of Alaska Fairbanks, William A. Egan Papers, UAF-1985-120-91; P.107, Alaska State Library, Evan Hill Collection, ASL-P343-411; P.108, University of Alaska Fairbanks, William A. Egan Papers, UAF-1985-120-103; P.109, University of Alaska Fairbanks, William A. Egan Papers, UAF-1985-120-474; P.110, Anchorage Museum of History & Art, Ward W. Wells, AMRC-wwc-19-1.

CHAPTER 8: THE FLYING BARITONE FROM FAIRBANKS

P.112, University of Alaska Fairbanks, Panoramas, UAF-1988-51-12; P.113, University of Alaska Fairbanks, Albert Johnson Collection, UAF-1989-166-165; P.114, University of Alaska Fairbanks, Cecil H. Kornegay Collection, UAF-1999-204-1; P.115, Courtesy U.S. Air Force; P.116, Courtesy NASA.

CHAPTER 9: J. DOOLITTLE: NOME TOWN BOY

P.118, Anchorage Museum of History and Art, O.D. Goetze Collection, AMRC-b01-41-62; P.119, Alaska State Library, P.E. Larss Collection, ASL-P41-154; P.120, Aunt Phil's Files; P.121, Anchorage Museum of History and Art, O.D. Goetze Collection, AMRC-b01-41-84; P.122, Alaska State Library, Portrait File, ASL-P01-1929; P.123, Aunt Phil's Files; P.124, Courtesy University of Texas Dallas; P.125, Courtesy U.S. Air Force.

CHAPTER 10: DUTCH HARBOR ATTACKED

P.126, Courtesy Library of Congress; P.127, Aunt Phil's Files; P.128a, Alaska State Library, H. Marion Thornton, ASL-P338-0053; P.128b, Alaska State Library, Aleutian/Pribilof Project Collection, ASL-P233-v150; P.129a, University of Alaska Fairbanks, San Francisco Call-Bulletin, UAF-1970-11-20; P.129b, University of Alaska Fairbanks, San Francisco Call-Bulletin, UAF-1970-11-18; P.130, Alaska State Library, H. Marion Thornton, ASL-P338-0529; P.131, Courtesy U.S. Naval Historical Center, NH 102457; P.132, Alaska State Library, James S. Russell Collection, ASL-P98-41; P.133, Alaska State Library, Aleutian/Pribilof Project, ASL-P233-v110.

CHAPTER 11: ENEMY INVADES ATTU

P.134, Courtesy National Park Service; P.135, University of Alaska Fairbanks, San Francisco Call-Bulletin, UAF-1970-11-22; P.136, Alaska State Library, Aleutian/Pribilof Project, ASL-P233-v133; P.137, University of Alaska Fairbanks, San Francisco Call-Bulletin, UAF-1970-11-66; P.138, University of Alaska Fairbanks, San Francisco Call-Bulletin, UAF-1970-11-71; P.139, University of Alaska Fairbanks, San Francisco Call-Bulletin, UAF-1970-11-53.

CHAPTER 12: JAPANESE-AMERICANS INTERRED

P.141, University of Washington, Social Issues Collection, SOC332; P.142, Courtesy National Park Service; P.143, University of Washington, Wing Luke Asian Museum Collection, 1992.041.004 AU; P.144, Courtesy National Park Service;

CHAPTER 13: ALEUTS BECOME REFUGEES

P.146, Alaska State Library, J. Simpson MacKinnon, ASL-P80-039; P.147, Anchorage Museum of History and Art, General Photograph File, AMRC-b78-104-4; P.148, Alaska State Library, Evan Hill Collection, ASL-P343-463; P.149, Alaska State Library, Evelyn Butler and George Dale, ASL-P306-1034; P.150, Alaska State Library, William R. Norton, ASL-P226-441; P.151, Alaska State Library, Winter & Pond, ASL-P87-0394; P.152, Alaska State Library, Evelyn Butler and George Dale, ASL-P306-1094; P.153, Alaska State Library, Evelyn Butler and George Dale, ASL-P306-1028; P.154, Alaska State Library, H. Marion Thornton, ASL-P338-0501; P.155, Alaska State Library, Evelyn Butler and George Dale, ASL-P306-2265; P.156, Alaska State Library, Evelyn Butler and George Dale, ASL-P306-1063; P.157a, Alaska State Library, Evelyn Butler and George Dale, ASL-P306-1099; P.157b, Alaska State Library, Evelyn Butler and George Dale, ASL-P306-1092; P.158, Alaska State Library, Evelyn Butler and George Dale, ASL-P306-1061; P.160, Alaska State Library, H. Marion Thornton, ASL-P338-1183; P.162a, Alaska State Library, Evan Hill, ASL-P343-429; P.162b, Alaska State Library, Evan Hill, ASL-P343-607; P.163a, Alaska State Library, Evan Hill, ASL-P343-424; P.163b, Alaska State Library, Evan Hill, ASL-P343-426; P.164, Alaska

State Library, Evan Hill, ASL-P343-433; P.165, Alaska State Library, Evan Hill Collection, ASL-P343-345; P.166, Alaska State Library, H. Marion Thornton, ASL-P338-0622; P.167, Alaska State Library, Place File, ASL-P0I-3749; P.168, University of Alaska Fairbanks, Floyd Akin, UAF-1978-133-154;

CHAPTER 14: ENEMY OUSTED FROM ALEUTIANS
P.170, University of Alaska Fairbanks, San Francisco Call-Bulletin, UAF-1970-11-30; P.172a, University of Alaska Fairbanks, San Francisco Call-Bulletin, UAF-1970-11-56; P.172b, University of Washington, Alaska-Western Canada, AWC0137; P.173, San Francisco Call-Bulletin, 1942-1948, UAF-1970-11-32; P.174a, University of Alaska Fairbanks, San Francisco Call-Bulletin, UAF-1970-11-46; P.174b, University of Alaska Fairbanks, San Francisco Call-Bulletin, UAF-1970-11-41; P.175, Alaska State Library, U.S. Army Signal Corps, ASL-P175-111; P.176a, Alaska State Library, U.S. Army Signal Corps, ASL-P175-112; P.176b, Alaska State Library, The Army in Alaska, ASL-P008-35; P.177a, University of Alaska Fairbanks, San Francisco Call-Bulletin, UAF-1970-11-34; P.177b, University of Alaska Fairbanks, San Francisco Call-Bulletin, UAF-1970-11-47; P.178, University of Alaska Fairbanks, San Francisco Call-Bulletin, UAF-1970-11-49; P.179, Anchorage Museum of History and Art, General Photograph File, AMRC-b80-75-29; P.180a, University of Alaska Fairbanks, San Francisco Call-Bulletin, UAF-1970-11-70; P.180b, Alaska State Library, H. Marion Thornton, ASL-P338-0635; P.181, Alaska State Library, U.S. Army Signal Corps, ASL-P175-146.

CHAPTER 15: 1945: DISCRIMINATION TORPEDOED
P.182, Alaska State Library, Winter and Pond, ASL-P87-1050; P.183, University of Alaska Anchorage, Howard and Mabel Jonish, UAA-hmc-0428-series5-f1-1; P.184, Alaska State Library, Documents, ASL-NomeNugget-March 3, 1944; P.186, Alaska State Library, Alaska Native Organizations, ASL-P33-01; P.187, Alaska State Library, Ed Andrews, ASL-P162-96; P.188, Alaska State Library, Portrait File, ASL-P0I-2568; P.189, Alaska State Library, Alaska Native Organizations, ASL-P33-19; P.190, Alaska State Library, Portrait File, ASL-P0I-3294; P.191, Alaska State Library, Documents, ASL-JuneauEmpire-February 6, 1945; P.192, Anchorage Museum of History and Art, General Photograph File, AMRC-b92-16-3.

CHAPTER 16: REEVE AIRWAYS TAKES FLIGHT
P.193, University of Alaska Anchorage, Russell W. Dow, UAA-hmc-0396-14f-185; P.194, University of Alaska Fairbanks, Kay J. Kennedy Aviation Collection, UAF-1991-98-137; P.195, University of Alaska Fairbanks, Kay J. Kennedy Aviation, UAF-1991-98-141; P.196, University of Alaska Anchorage, Russell W. Dow, UAA-hmc-0396-14f-59; P.197, University of Alaska Fairbanks, Kay J. Kennedy Aviation, UAF-1991-98-140; P.198a, Aunt Phil's Files; P.198b, Alaska State Library, Alaska Dept. Health & Social Services, ASL-P143-0095; P.199, Anchorage Museum of History & Art, General Photograph File, AMRC-b91-19-92.

CHAPTER 17: 1948: MURDERER NOMINATED KING
P.201, Anchorage Museum of History & Art, General Photograph File, AMRC-b77-5-4; P.202, University of Alaska Fairbanks, RC Force Papers, UAF-2003-174-328; P.203a, Courtesy National Archives, Pacific Alaska Region; P.203b, Anchorage Museum of History & Art, Ward W. Wells, AMRC-wws-1787; P.204, Anchorage Museum of History & Art,

John Urban Collection, AMRC-b64-1-736; P.205a, Aunt Phil's Files; P.205b, University of Washington Libraries, Asahel Curtis Collection, CUR595; P.206, Courtesy Anchorage Daily Times; P.207, Courtesy National Archives, Pacific Alaska Region.

CHAPTER 18: 1948: ALASKA AIRLINES MAKES HISTORY
P.209, University of Alaska Fairbanks, Kay J. Kennedy Aviation, UAF-1991-98-87; P.210, University of Alaska Fairbanks, Kay J. Kennedy Aviation, UAF-1991-98-587; P.212, Courtesy National Archives; P.213, Courtesy U.S. Air Force; P.214, Courtesy Israeli National Photo Collection; P.215a, Alaska State Library, Lloyd Jarman, ASL-P337-09-007; P.215b, Alaska State Library, Lloyd Jarman, ASL-P337-03-203; P.216, Alaska Coastal, Alaska State Library, Sheldon B. Simmons, Alaska Airlines & Aviation, ASL-P356-107; P.217, University of Alaska Anchorage, Donald Arthur Post, UAA-hmc-0917-833.

CHAPTER 19: IN OTHER NEWS ...
P.219, Alaska State Library, Portrait File, ASL-P01-4380; P.220, Alaska State Library, Evelyn Butler and George Dale, ASL-P306-0760; P.221a, Aunt Phil's Files; P.221b, Alaska State Library, Evelyn Butler and George Dale, ASL-P306-0793; P.222, Aunt Phil's Files; P.223, Alaska State Library, Evelyn Butler and George Dale, ASL-P306-0271; P.224, Alaska State Library, Alaska Dept. of Health & Social Services, ASL-P143-0983; P.225, Alaska State Library, Case and Draper, ASL-P39-0656; P.226a, Alaska State Library, William R. Norton, ASL-P226-427; P.226b, Courtesy National Park Service; P.227a, University of Alaska Anchorage, Christine M. McClain, UAA-hmc-0370-series15b-30-17-4; P.227b, University of Alaska Anchorage, Peter Dinkelspiel Alaska Highway Photo Album, UAA-hmc-0470-series1-56.

CHAPTER 20: 'RED SCARE' BRINGS BOOM
P.228, Museum of History & Industry, Seattle, Seattle Post-Intelligencer, 1986.5.2106.1; P.229, University of Alaska Anchorage, Christine M. McClain, UAA-hmc-0370-series15a-2-105; 230a, University of Alaska Anchorage, Crystal and Ray Williams, UAA-hmc-0549-7c; P.230b, University of Alaska Anchorage, Christine M. McClain, UAA-hmc-0370-series15b-30-4; P.232, Anchorage Museum of History & Art, Wien Collection, AMRC-b85-27-1039; P.233a, Anchorage Museum of History & Art, Wien Collection, AMRC-b85-27-1226; P.233b, Courtesy U.S. Air Force; P.234, University of Alaska Fairbanks, Walter W. Hodge, UAF-2003-63-57; P.235, University of Alaska Anchorage, Donald Arthur Post Slides, UAA-hmc-0917-450.

CHAPTER 21: ANCHORAGE: JEWEL ON THE TUNDRA
P.236, Anchorage Museum of History & Art, General Photograph File, AMRC-b76-82-33; P.237, University of Alaska Fairbanks, Walter W. Hodge, UAF-2003-63-68; P.238, University of Alaska Anchorage, Benzie Ola Dow, UAA-hmc-0397-11k-29-10; P.240a, Anchorage Museum of History & Art, General Photograph File, AMRC-b96-4-49; P.240b, Anchorage Museum of History & Art, Ward W. Wells, AMRC-wws-3292; P.241a, Anchorage Museum of History & Art, General Photograph File, AMRC-b76-82-30; P.241b, Russell W. Dow, University of Alaska Anchorage, UAA-hmc-0396-14o-f4-12; P.242, Anchorage Museum of History and Art, General Photograph File, AMRC-b76-82-45; P.243, Anchorage Museum

of History & Art, General Photograph File, AMRC-b76-82-101; P.244a, Anchorage Museum of History & Art, Ward W. Wells, AMRC-wwc-1288; P.244b, University of Alaska Anchorage, Donald Arthur Post Slides, UAA-hmc-0917-713; P.245a, Anchorage Museum of History & Art, Ward W. Wells Collection, AMRC-wwc-7462; P.245b, Anchorage Museum of History & Art, Ward W. Wells, AMRC-wws-3016-50; P.246, Anchorage Museum of History & Art, Ward W. Wells, AMRC-wws-3444-13; P.247, Anchorage Museum of History & Art, Wien Collection, AMRC-b85-27-791; P.248, Anchorage Museum of History & Art, Wien Collection, AMRC-b85-27-813; P.249, Anchorage Museum of History & Art, Ward W. Wells, AMRC-wws-3145; P.250, Anchorage Museum of History & Art, Ward W. Wells, AMRC-wwc-1985-5.

CHAPTER 22: OTHER ALASKA TOWNS GROW

P.251, University of Alaska Fairbanks, Cecil H. Kornegay, UAF-1999-204-17; P.252, University of Alaska Fairbanks, Cecil H. Kornegay, UAF-1999-204-94; P.253, University of Alaska Fairbanks, Ceci H. Kornegay, UAF-1999-204-98; P.254a, University of Alaska Anchorage, Donald Arthur Post, UAA-hmc-0917-596; P.254b, University of Alaska Anchorage, Seward Church of Christ, UAA-hmc-0632-23b; P.255a, Anchorage Museum of History & Art, General Photograph File, AMRC-b71-x-5-13; P.255b, Anchorage Museum of History & Art, General Photograph File, AMRC-b71-x-5-19; P.256a, University of Alaska Anchorage, Russell W. Dow, UAA-hmc-0396-14f-193; P.256b, University of Alaska Anchorage, Hans and Margaret Hafemeister, UAA-hmc-0126-m1-2-39; P.257a, Alaska State Library, Winter and Pond, ASL-P87-1007; P.257b, Anchorage Museum of History & Art, Ickes Collection, AMRC-b75-175-598; P.258a, Alaska State Library, Dora M. Sweeney, ASL-P421-280; P.258b, Alaska State Library, Winter and Pond, ASL-P87-1496; P.259a, University of Alaska Anchorage, Christine M. McClain, UAA-hmc-0370-series15b-33-19-1; P.259b, Alaska State Library, Ed Andrews, ASL-P162-053.

CHAPTER 23: TUBERCULOSIS: THE ALASKA SCOURGE

P.260, Anchorage Museum of History & Art, Ickes Collection, AMRC-b75-175-522; P.261, Alaska State Library, Alaska Dept. of Health & Social Services, ASL-P143-1010; P.262, Alaska State Library, Leslie Melvin, ASL-P222-0353; P.263, University of Alaska Fairbanks, Anthony J. Dimond, UAF-1992-90-7; P.264a, Alaska State Library, Alaska Dept. of Health & Social Services, ASL-P143-0291; P.264b, Anchorage Museum of History & Art, General Photograph File, AMRC-b94-11-4; P.265, Alaska State Library, Alaska Dept. of Health & Social Services, ASL-P143-0283; P.266, Alaska State Library, Rev. Samuel Spriggs, ASL-P320-05; P.267a, Anchorage Museum of History & Art, Ward W. Wells, AMRC-wws-1420-1; P.267, Alaska State Library, Alaska Dept. of Health & Social Services, ASL-P143-0506; P.268, University of Alaska Anchorage, C. Earl Albrecht, UAA-hmc-0375-pArtl-series1c-23-1; P.269, Alaska State Library, Alaska Dept. of Health & Social Services, ASL-P143-0238; P.270, Alaska State Library, Alaska Dept. of Health & Social Services, ASL-P143-1282.

CHAPTER 24: EARLY MOVERS & SHAKERS

P.272, University of Alaska Anchorage, National Geographic Society Katmai Expeditions, UAA-hmc-0186-volume3-1021; P.273, Alaska State Library, Winter and Pond, ASL-P87-2429; P.274, Alaska State Library, Wickersham State Historic Site, ASL-P277-019-024;

P.275, Alaska State Library, Portrait File, ASL-P01-1278; P.276a, University of Alaska Fairbanks, Anthony J. Dimond Papers, UAF-1992-90-17; P.276b, Alaska State Library, Doyle C. Tripp, ASL-P454-047.

CHAPTER 25: STATEHOOD MOMENTUM BUILDS
P.278, University of Alaska Fairbanks, Vertical File-Individuals, UAF-1978-138-14; P.269, University of Alaska Fairbanks, Ernest F. Jessen Cartoons, UAF-2001-139-10; P.280, University of Alaska Fairbanks, Cecil H. Kornegay, UAF-1999-204-3; P.281a, University of Alaska Fairbanks, Ernest H. Gruening Papers, UAF-1976-21-55145; P.281b, University of Alaska Fairbanks, Edward Lewis Bartlett Papers, UAF-1990-176-241; P.282, University of Alaska Anchorage, Ferrall W. Campbell Papers, UAA-hmc-0364-series5-3-8; P.283a, University of Alaska Fairbanks, Edward Lewis Bartlett Papers, UAF-1990-176-352; P.283b, University of Alaska Anchorage, Marie Silverman APU Collection, UAA-hmc-0778-5-16; P.284, University of Alaska Fairbanks, Ernest H. Gruening Papers, UAF-1976-21-854; P.285, University of Alaska Fairbanks, Ernest F. Jessen Cartoons, UAF-2001-139-11; P.286, University of Alaska Fairbanks, Constitutional Convention Delegate Photographs, UAF-1968-16-1.

CHAPTER 26: EGAN: THE FINAL PUSH
P.287, University of Alaska Fairbanks, William A. Egan Papers, UAF-1985-120-364; P.288, Alaska State Library, Portrait File, ASL-CPO-Groups-Legislature-1950s-03; P.289, University of Alaska Fairbanks, Constitutional Convention Delegate Photographs, UAF-1983-185-18; P.290, Alaska State Library, Documents, ASL-J87.A417G89; P.292, University of Alaska Fairbanks, William A. Egan, UAF-1985-120-259; P.293, Alaska State Library, Subject File, ASL-AlaskaStatehood-9.

CHAPTER 27: BLACK GOLD TIPS THE BALANCE
P.295, Alaska State Library, Alaska Division of Tourism, ASL-P22-06-068; P.296, Alaska State Library, Ray W. Moss, ASL-P11-074; P.297, University of Alaska Fairbanks, Barrett Willoughby, UAF-1972-116-180; P.298a, University of Alaska Fairbanks, Barrett Willoughby, UAF-1972-116-152; P.298b, Anchorage Museum of History & Art, General Photograph File, AMRC-b89-14-42; P.299, University of Alaska Fairbanks, Barrett Willoughby, UAF-1972-116-213; P.300, Alaska State Library, Alaska Division of Tourism, ASL-P22-06-069; P.301, University of Alaska Fairbanks, Barrett Willoughby, UAF-1972-116-212.

CHAPTER 28: WE'RE IN!
P.302, Anchorage Museum of History & Art, Ward W. Wells, AMRC-wwc-6725-12; P.303, Statehood A-1, Anchorage Daily Times; P.304a, Anchorage Museum of History & Art, Ward W. Wells, AMRC-wws-2023-6; P.304b, Anchorage Museum of History & Art, Ward W. Wells, AMRC-wws-2023-41; P.305, University of Alaska Fairbanks, Ernest H. Gruening Papers, UAF-1976-21-55334; P.306, University of Alaska Fairbanks, Ernest H. Gruening Papers, UAF-1976-21-1301; P.308, University of Alaska Fairbanks, Ernest H. Gruening Papers, UAF-1976-21-289; P.309, Anchorage Museum of History & Art, Ward W. Wells, AMRC-wws-2018-36; P.310, Alaska State Library, Candace Waugaman, ASL-P379-283; P.311, University of Alaska Fairbanks, Ernest H. Gruening, UAF-1976-21-281;

P.312, Anchorage Museum of History & Art, General Photograph File, AMRC-b82-66-3; P.313a, Alaska State Library, Caroline Jensen, ASL-P417-024; P.313b, University of Alaska Fairbanks, Ernest H. Gruening Papers, UAF-1976-21-57312; P.314, University of Alaska Fairbanks, Ralph J. Rivers Papers, UAF-1972-49-161; P.315, Alaska State Library, Winter and Pond, ASL-P87-0896; P.316a, University of Alaska Fairbanks, William A. Egan Papers, UAF-1985-120-192; P.316b, University of Alaska Fairbanks, Ernest H. Gruening Papers, UAF-1976-21-57235; P.317, University of Alaska Fairbanks, Ernest Gruening Papers, UAF-1976-21-77747.

CHAPTER 29: 'SIMPLE FLAG OF THE LAST FRONTIER'
P.318, Alaska State Library, C.L. Andrews Collection, ASL-PCA-45-346; P.319, Aunt Phil's Files; P.320, Anchorage Museum of History and Art, General Photograph File, AMRC-b74-40-119; P.321, Alaska State Library, American Legion Collection, ASL-MS14-1; P.322, Alaska State Library, Portrait File, ASL-P01-1921; P.323, Alaska State Library, George A. Parks Collection, ASL-P240-191; P.324, University of Alaska Fairbanks, William A. Egan papers, UAF-1985-120-135; P.325, Courtesy NASA; P.326, Alaska State Library, Portrait File, ASL-P01-0402.

PREVIEW VOLUME 5
P.343a, Anchorage Museum of History & Art, General Photograph File, AMRC-b70-15-33; P.343b, University of Washington, Alaska and Western Canada, AWC0610; P.344a, University of Alaska Anchorage, Alfred & Mae Bakken, UAA-hmc-0589-1-56; 344b, Alaska State Library, Trans-Alaska Pipeline Construction, ASL-P002-6-14; P.344c, Courtesy of NOAA.

Preview Of Aunt Phil's Trunk: Volume 5

Earthquake!

The Great Alaska Earthquake struck on Good Friday, March 27, 1964, at 5:36 p.m. It registered 8.6 on the Richter Scale, although scientists now favor a different magnitude scale for large quakes that shows it as 9.2.

Many Alaska communities, such as Seward – seen above – were heavily damaged by fires and the tsunami that followed the quake.

Downtown Anchorage, pictured below, was especially hard hit. Building façades crashed into the street. In some places one side of the street dropped more than 10 feet.

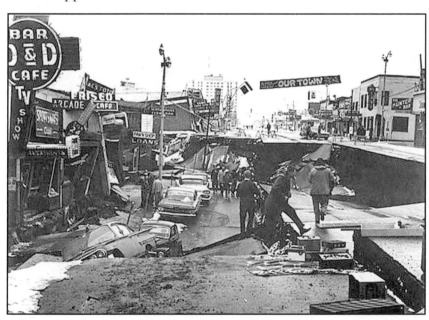

Flood!

Water spilled over the banks of the Chena River and rushed into downtown Fairbanks on Aug. 20, 1967. Flood waters filled the city's streets, submerged cars and sent debris throughout the area.

Oil Discovered!

Following a massive oil discovery on Alaska's North Slope in the late 1960s, trans-Alaska oil pipeline workers began laying 800 miles of pipe in March 1975. The $8 billion project crossed three mountain ranges and 800 waterways.

Oil Spilled!

Just after midnight on March 24, 1989, the single-hulled oil tanker *Exxon Valdez* ran aground on Bligh Reef in Prince William Sound. Almost 11 million gallons of North Slope crude spilled.